Perfect lighting

To my children, Lucca, Cazalla, and Alexander,
and my wonderful husband, Christopher

CRE▲TIVE
HOMEOWNER

PERFECT LIGHTING

Inspiring solutions for every room

SALLY STOREY

Photography by Luke White

First Published in North America in 2008 by

CREATIVE
HOMEOWNER®

Creative Homeowner® is a resistered trademark
of Federal Marketing Corporation

Perfect Lighting
ISBN 10: 1-58011-417-2
ISBN 13: 978-1-58011-417-2
Library of Congress Control Number: 2008922039

Current printing (last digit)
10 9 8 7 6 5 4 3 2 1

Originally published in Great Britain in 2008 by
Jacqui Small, 7 Greenland Street, London NW1 0ND

Publisher Jacqui Small
Commissioning Editor Joanna Copestick
Art Director Lawrence Morton
Project Editor Zia Mattocks
Production Peter Colley

Printed and bound in Singapore

CREATIVE HOMEOWNER
A Division of Federal Marketing Corp.
24 Park Way
Upper Saddle River, NJ 07458

www.creativehomeowner.com

RIGHT Light plays an important part in lighting spaces.
In the foreground, the softly shaded pendant hovers
over the table, creating a warm glow. The dramatically
backlit shelves have double the impact as they reflect
on the polished wooden table. The eye is drawn into
the living room beyond by the continuous light over the
curtains, which provides a visual focus at night. This
image plays on many of the aspects introduced in this
book, including the layering of light, reflecting light,
creating focus, and using light as an architectural tool.

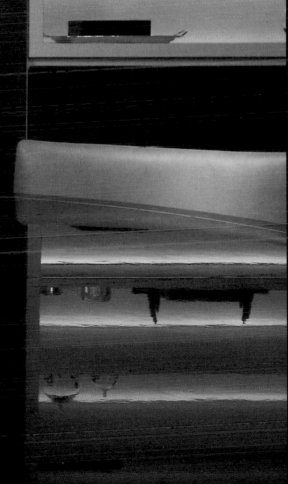

Introduction 8

What lighting can do 12

Enhance space 14
Define features 24
Decorate surfaces 30
Create contrast 36
Set the mood 40
Add drama 46

Lighting at work 52

Background lighting 54
Accent lighting 60
Concealed lighting 66
Task lighting 72
Decorative lighting 76
Layering 94

Lighting in practice: room by room 100

Living rooms 102
Kitchens 110
Dining areas 118
Bedrooms 122
Bathrooms 130
Working areas 138
Halls, corridors, stairs, and landings 142
Pathways, exteriors, and entrances 146
Outdoor entertaining 150
Gardens, decks, and landscaping 154
Poolscapes 158

Hardware 160

Lighting tool box 162
Pendants and chandeliers 164
Floor lamps 166
Table lamps 167
Wall lights 168
Task lights 169
Practicalities 170

Glossary 172
Suppliers 173
Index 175
Acknowledgments 176

asuccessful, innovative lighting scheme can bring a house to life, enhancing the space, providing a sense of drama, and creating pools of focus around furniture, architectural features, and on walls and floors. Too often lighting comes bottom of the list when it comes to designing a house, and it is only when the decoration of a room is almost finished that it becomes obvious that the lights are not in the right place—whether for reading, lighting a painting, or showing off the interior architecture. The ideal time to plan a lighting scheme is right at the start of a home-renovation or new building. It is vital that lighting design be considered at the earliest stages, around the same time as the plumbing work is being undertaken.

For this reason, before you begin to plan the lighting, it is essential that you make decisions about the layout of furniture and pictures. Sometimes there is more than one possible furniture arrangement, in which case the key is to design the lighting to suit alternative configurations. This may only mean that a couple of extra receptacles are needed, but it is far better and less expensive in the long run to provide for this early on, rather than try to put it right once the scheme is complete. Always provide enough receptacles in the corners of living rooms, because additional lighting is very often required for lamps and plug-in uplights. In large rooms, receptacles may also be required in the center of the room; these can be recessed in the floor and hidden underneath sofas or other pieces of furniture.

When planning a successful lighting scheme, it is invaluable to have an appreciation of what can be achieved with light through careful direction and control, together with a considered balance of different light sources used at various intensities for maximum flexibility. All of these elements come into play when creating a variety of effects. In this book basic lighting

PREVIOUS PAGES By day and by night, light manipulates this living space. During the day, the natural light floods into the room and lights the reveals of the windows. By night, the same effect is achieved with uplights to each reveal, creating contrast with the other walls. At night, the soft light under the unit on the left, which reflects off the wooden floor, adds a lamplike quality. The stairs are unlit during the day, but at night they become a central focus, internally illuminated using white LEDs.

> "The most successful lighting is discreet and brings out the best in an interior or garden, while badly planned lighting will often be glaring and will show everything at its worst."

principles are explained in "What lighting can do," on page 12. Armed with this knowledge, you can explore how these effects can be put to practical use within the home in "Lighting at work," on page 52. When planning a scheme, the main points to consider are the task lighting (for reading in bed or for preparing food in the kitchen, for example), the general, background lighting and, finally, the accent lighting that creates the main design interest and focus. All of these aspects need to be considered for each room, but the solutions will usually vary depending on the type of room and its purpose. The key lighting requirements of the main rooms in the home are discussed in "Lighting in practice," on page 100.

Variety is important for creating interest, so try to employ several lighting effects, just as you would when choosing a mix of textures and colors for a decoration scheme. Mix uplights with downlights for task, background, and accent lighting; then connect them to different circuits to allow for changes in mood. In a living room, it is more useful to create background and task lighting with freestanding lamps, but provide accent lighting with recessed spots to highlight favorite pictures, or a very narrow-beam lamp (bulb) downlighting flowers on a coffee table to create a focal point. For an additional layer of light, consider installing discreet lights within a niche or shelving unit. Shelf lighting brings effective punctuation to a space, whether it is enlivening a kitchen display, bookcases in a living room, or bathroom accessories. The creative possibilities are endless, using frontlighting, backlighting, downlighting, or edge-lighting. Shelving can be lit horizontally or vertically, too, for an extra dimension. Introduce drama by highlighting a room's architectural features, such as a large open fireplace, an arched doorway, or a column. Stunning effects can be created by lighting columns with a light recessed into the floor, close to the base, so the light will graze up the side and produce dramatic focus at the top. If additional light is needed, try using a low-level uplight instead of a freestanding lamp. This will create a soft pool of flattering uplight in the corners of a room. A similar technique can be used behind a sofa in a bay window to uplight the curtains.

Lighting a less-obvious space can add unexpected drama. If you light a half-landing leading off an entrance hall, for example, your eye will be drawn to the brightest point, creating a sense of flow between the areas and increasing the feeling of space. In the same way, if the garden or space beyond a window is lit, the external lighting will draw the eye outside, effectively making it feel like an extension of the interior. This also prevents the window from acting like a mirror at night and reflecting everything in the room.

When using downlights in a space for general light, try to avoid positioning them directly above where people's heads are likely to be because this produces uncomfortable and unflattering results. Instead, use directional downlights to light walls or cupboards, then the general light becomes softer and more reflected. If you are using low-voltage downlights, avoid symmetrical ceiling layouts and straight lines of downlights, which can produce a sterile "office" feel. Think about what you want to light, and focus the downlight on that object—whether the center of a picture or over a dining table.

Control is crucial for flexible lighting schemes, so always fit dimmers so that you can alter the ambiance of the room; having more than one dimmer will allow you a wider choice of lighting effects. For example, put your table lamps on one circuit, low-voltage downlights emphasizing pictures on a second, and downlights focusing on the center of a table on a third. The accent lighting will not be required all the time and should always be on a separate switch and dimmer so that you can achieve different moods. All lamps and uplights are best placed on a 15- or 20-amp lighting circuit controlled by dimmer switches by the door, allowing you to switch them all on or off at one time and offering the potential to dim them to create different moods. If the room is already wired, there are various radio-frequency control products that allow a dimmer wired in the base of a table lamp to be linked with other lamps and a switch by the door.

Light sources in most houses are typically low-voltage halogen for downlights and traditional incandescent bulbs for lamps. Increasingly, these are being replaced with new, warm, energy-efficient compact fluorescents and LEDs (light emitting diodes) for discreet decorative effects, such as color-changing or shelf and step features, or for use as decking indicator lights. Incandescent light is yellow, warm, and inviting, while halogen has a crisp white color that works as a supplement to daylight in dark rooms, particularly in lower and ground-floor areas. Its other advantage is its small lamp size, which enables the use of neater, unobtrusive fixtures. The concealing of light fixtures is an important process when creating a successful lighting scheme. The key is to choose downlights that conceal the lamp, as the eye is always drawn to the brightest point. If the lamp is well recessed in its fixture, the object that is lit will become the key focus, rather than the light source itself. Or conceal the light source by creating a recess in a wall in which to install the downlights. This works well in a contemporary interior, creating an architectural effect, like a wall light (see pages 23 and 144). For the best results, be bold, have fun, and remember these golden rules of lighting: design layers of interesting effects and use low-glare fixtures to conceal the light sources.

WHAT LIGHTING CAN DO

Lighting is a powerful and versatile design tool that can be used in many different ways to enhance interiors and bring a home to life. In addition to being a functional necessity by providing light for practical purposes, lighting can be used to create zones and points of focus, to manipulate the dimensions of a space, to draw attention to an architectural feature, or to add a decorative element—whether by creating a pattern, highlighting an interesting surface, or providing a dramatic effect through the play of light and shadow.

Enhance space

Lighting can be used to manipulate space in many ways, whether by increasing the sense of volume, improving the proportions of a room, linking areas together, or defining zones in an open-plan space by creating points of focus.

proportion, scale, and volume

As lighting governs what we see, it is probably one of the most important elements in determining how we view a room. Lighting can create a feeling of space and volume, or warmth and intimacy. It can be used to reinforce the architectural statement and emphasize proportion. For example, a series of columns can be uplit with narrow-beam lights to make them appear taller.

Light works by reflecting off a surface. It will reflect more off a very light surface and be able to play more tricks of spaciousness and brightness than it can off a black or dark-colored surface. A dark room will absorb the light and will never appear bright, however much it is lit. A white room, on the other hand, can really be manipulated by light and made to seem intimate and dramatic, or bright and airy. If a white room is downlit and the walls remain unlit, so that the only light is that which is reflected off the floor, the full potential of the space will not be realized. However, if you take the emphasis off the floor and "wash" the walls with light, the space will seem brighter and more spacious. Lighting two opposite walls will make the other two unlit walls appear darker, making the room seem wider even if it is perfectly square. In addition, the walls that are lit will seem to be a different shade of white from those that are in shadow, even though they are exactly the same.

Uplighting a room has a similar effect on a room's dimensions to wall washing. It provides a very diffuse light and usually increases the feeling of volume, making a room seem more spacious and creating a sense of airiness by reflecting light off the ceiling. A space lit indirectly in this way is softer and provides a nicer environment to be in than one lit by straightforward downlighting, which should be kept for task-orientated solutions and for creating focus.

Uplighting can be achieved from the walls, floor, and even freestanding furniture within a room. The best solution depends on the height of the room. For uplighting to be effective, the light needs to spread; the light source should not be too close to the ceiling, but it must be above eye level to avoid glare. For this reason, there is no point installing wall uplights in a room with

ABOVE This dramatic archway frames the entrance to a dark lobby. The large chandelier provides a strong visual focus of light in a conventional way and is dimmed so that the candle lamps do not create too much glare. Its size gives a sense of grandeur to the space. The arch itself is uplit using low-voltage low-heat uplights to emphasize the strong architectural detail. This acts as a wonderful foil to the traditional chandelier.

OPPOSITE A glass balustrade separates the television room, seen from the glass bridge, from the double-height living room below. A very soft, relaxing light was required to create a welcoming feel, but with very few (if any) table lamps. The solution was four discreet low-voltage directional downlights, which provide a soft light reflected off the white walls. To introduce another soft element of light similar in quality to lamp light, a linear light source was mounted behind the 2-in.-thick (50mm) shelves of the bookcases that frame the sofa on either side, imparting a gentle backlight.

"More light is reflected off a light surface than a dark one, so a white or pale room will be brighter with a greater sense of spaciousness."

BELOW AND BELOW RIGHT This dining room, seen at night, illustrates how lighting the exterior can make the interior space seem larger, as the eye travels through the window to the lit landscape beyond it. When the garden is unlit, the windows act almost as a mirror, reflecting the interior. The lighting within the room is very soft. The two large lamps that frame the fireplace give the visual focus. The specially designed picture light is traditional in style, with a slightly extended arm. It uses low-voltage lamps and lenses to ensure an even wash of light. Around the perimeter of the room, miniature low-voltage low-glare downlights provide a gentle wash and highlight the curtains. A narrow beam downlight is focused on the vase of flowers in the center of the table.

OPPOSITE This living room leads into a television room, and the lighting helps to tie the two spaces together. Soft background light is provided by the two chandeliers with cream shades, one in each space. A task light over the sofa is ideal for reading. Low-glare 10-deg. downlights provide focus on the coffee tables, and the bronze sculpture by Harry Bertoia is lit by a spotlight on the column.

a low ceiling. In this case, a better solution would be recessed floor uplights or a more diffuse light source, perhaps concealed by a piece of furniture.

In small, low spaces where it is difficult to uplight, sometimes the solution is to light the four corners of the room, using either recessed uplights or small portable lights placed behind an object. These are bright narrow-beam light sources and need to be baffled to avoid direct view. If recessed, then the source of light needs to have a narrow beam and should be recessed well within the fixture.

In a space with a sloping ceiling, such as a loft or attic room, a more diffuse uplight may be required because the narrow-beam effect will be too specific. A low-level light under frosted glass could be the solution. (See page 139.) For such a space, fluorescents, which can be overlapped to provide a continuous light, are ideal. For a different effect at night, a second row of fluorescents could be used, sleeved with a different color.

If you have built-in furniture and uplighting is impossible, consider using a glass-top table with light, or a large, round contemporary glow light. (See page 166.) These will provide all-over light, including uplight.

Another way to increase the perception of space is by lighting something beyond the room in question. A lit window box or balcony, for example, takes the eye beyond the window at night, extending the feeling of space. The same is true of lighting any external area. Similarly, in a narrow hall, lighting something beyond—such as an object or artwork on a staircase or half-landing, or a feature under a staircase—draws the eye to this area and creates a feeling of more space. (See page 58.)

defining areas and linking spaces

While light cannot physically divide a space, when different light intensities are used in different areas, lighting can be an effective tool in creating visual barriers and defining zones. This function of lighting becomes important in an open-plan space where different activities are carried out, such as a single-space loft apartment or a combined kitchen–family room. Large, open spaces such as these can seem cold and impersonal if uniformly lit, but using different light levels to separate areas and create distinct zones within the room imparts a cozy, inviting atmosphere.

Defining areas can be achieved in many ways—as much through a lack of light, creating areas of shadow, as through the use and drama of light. How it is done depends on the type of space and the kind of activities it supports. In an open-plan living area, for example, something as simple as a lit sculpture or even a vase of flowers thrown into focus can become a visual punctuation point, effectively dividing two areas from each other.

While well-considered lighting in the various zones of an open-plan layout creates pools of focus that imbue the space with a feeling of intimacy, in connected rooms—such as a master bedroom and bath, or a kitchen that opens onto a living or dining space—lighting can also be used to draw the eye

LEFT An important function of lighting is to create points of focus and pools of light to lead you through a space in stages. Here, the first room—a library—has been softly lit, with table lamps setting the mood. The shelving unit that frames the entrance into the living room is discreetly lit with concealed xenon low-voltage light strips along the front edges, creating columns of light that draw the eye through to the room beyond. The living room is lit in a traditional way with lamps, but the main focus is the fireplace, which is lit with two recessed uplights that highlight the detail of the fire surround. This unexpected effect that makes the fireplace come alive, even in the summer when the fire is not lit.

RIGHT This master bath and bedroom have been cleverly linked by means of a timber-louvered screen that has been uplit at the base to provide a soft indirect light. The light source is a series of small recessed fiber-optic uplights on both sides of the screen, so that when it is closed they still create interest by highlighting its surface. With the screen open, the eye is drawn through to the brightest point beyond: when you are in bed, the focus is the narrow low-voltage downlight on the wonderful stone bathtub; when you are in the bathroom, the focus becomes the lit pictures in the bedroom.

Top tips

If you are undertaking major building or home renovations, plan your lighting scheme at the same time as the plumbing, to ensure that you get the most from your scheme.

Before you make any decisions, consider all the uses that will be made of the room and the kind of activities it will need to support at different times of the day.

When using low-voltage downlights, think about what you want to light, and focus the downlight in the center of a picture or over a table. Don't create symmetrical lines of lights.

Layer lights at different levels to build up a palette of effects. Use a combination of low-level uplights, wall-recessed floor washers, and individual lights for shelves and niches.

Don't be afraid to combine traditional lighting effects with modern solutions, such as a decorative chandelier with discreet, hardworking downlights.

BELOW This large open-plan living area is effectively subdivided by light. Each area is treated in its own way, and the pools of light and different focuses create impact. On both sides of the room are stairs leading to bedrooms, and the walls behind are lit using 100-watt, 12-volt lamps in dedicated wall-wash reflectors, which produce an even light without the usual arcs. This brings the walls into strong focus, and the reflected light adds to the general illumination. The large pendants suspended low over the dining table help to reduce the scale of the room. The light from them is dimmed and infilled by the soft wall wash at either end, while the table is highlighted by three narrow 4-deg. recessed spotlights above it. The strong visual focus in the center of the space, which links all the areas together, is the stone sculpture lit from above and slightly to the side with a narrow-beam light source.

through to the area beyond it, increasing the sense of space by making the rooms flow easily one into the other.

Not to be forgotten are the internal linking zones, the halls and corridors that physically join rooms together. These are the roads within a home, but they are often at the bottom of the list when it comes to considering design and lighting. Because these spaces are generally not cluttered with furniture, they can provide the opportunity for the most creative lighting effects. In a hall with a low ceiling, lighting the floor with recessed low-level floor washers makes the passage exciting, rather than bland and boring. The recent advancements in the development of low-energy LED sources mean that this can be a practical, cost-effective lighting solution that can be left on all night. (See also pages 142–5.)

The lighting in connecting areas, whether between adjoining rooms or a room and an internal linking zone, needs to share the same level of control and subtlety so that the ambiance can be set in both areas. There is no point having a moody and dramatic living room, for example, if the hall it opens onto is bright with no control. Besides, as light will always spill into the living room from the hall and provide an uneasy contrast.

ABOVE This bay window, which forms a seating area at the end of a bedroom, is flanked by shelves that are individually lit to add a soft indirect light to the room. Within the bay, three directional downlights create a strong pattern of light and shadow, emphasizing the horizontal lines of the Venetian blinds and, by contrast, the vertical columns of the drapes. The freestanding lamp with its handcrafted base and shade is like a sculpture in the space.

"By creating welcoming pools of light and points of focus that draw the eye, you can use lighting to help define zones in open spaces and link them together."

creating focus | When planning the lighting in any room, it is important to decide first what are the key focal points, so that they can be lit individually. They may include a favorite picture or sculpture, a piece of furniture, or an architectural feature that will benefit from being highlighted. The eye is always drawn to the brightest point, so focus is created by highlighting whatever you want to be a feature—the eye will naturally follow these "stepping stones" of light. When I create a lighting plan for a room, I color focal points yellow; if there is "too much yellow," I know there are too many focal points, and I need to be more selective to create impact. Lighting that is subtle and selective is often far more effective than too much.

Creating focus is about playing with contrast. If something is lit more strongly than its surroundings, then it will stand out; if the surroundings are dark, it will stand out even more. To create focus successfully, it is important to understand how the general lighting in the space is created—whether by table lamps, pendants, recessed downlights, uplights, or any number of combinations. This overall lighting needs to be controlled separately from the effects that create focus, so that these stand out when the general lighting is dimmed. Other key points to bear in mind is that the object or feature being lit must be the brightest point, and the light source must be shielded—if it is not, the light source becomes the brightest point that draws the eye, and not the intended feature.

LEFT There are three key "stepping stones" of light creating the focus in this space and leading the eye through it. The first is the traditional chandelier, which is dimmed but sets the mood. This is what first draws the eye and seems to be main source of light illuminating the archway. Less obvious, initially, is the impact created by the tiny recessed uplights at floor level, which highlight the detail on the arch. The eye is then drawn through the room and beyond the window to the lit urn at the end of the garden.

RIGHT The focus in this contemporary apartment's wide central hall is the art on the end wall. This focus is exaggerated by the contrast between the strongly lit picture and the surrounding dark timber space that is barely lit. Another effect that has worked well to increase the drama is the series of recessed slots, about 4 in. (100mm) square in section, fitted with a recessed uplight at the bottom and a downlight at the top. The vertical slots become almost wall lights, and the light effect seen on the wood floor is similar to that produced by floor washers.

> "The eye is drawn to the brightest point, so the key is to choose downlights that conceal the bulb—if the bulb is well recessed in its fixture, the object you are lighting rather than the light source will become the focus."

Define features

Lighting can be used to great effect to highlight points of interest in an interior, bringing out the detail of an architectural feature by uplighting a ceiling molding, accentuating the clean lines of a contemporary design by concealing a strip light in the ceiling, or lighting a display of art or a collection of objects.

architectural features

Lighting is an excellent tool for emphasizing and delineating the architectural features within a home. These features can then become the focus of the room. In a contemporary house, it may be the stairs, the effect of light on a wonderful material, the texture of a rough-hewn wall, or the recessed slots within a smooth wall giving a glimpse into another room. (See page 23.) In a traditional home, the highlighted features may be a column or an archway, a fireplace, or a staircase. Each element needs to be considered individually, to ensure that it is lit in such a way as to bring out its best features.

In a contemporary house, the lighting solution to highlight a wonderful material with a wall-wash effect could be to recess a light fixture into the ceiling at the top of the wall. Use a continuous light source such as xenon, an overlapping fluorescent, or an LED strip. This always provides more emphasis at the top of the wall, but has the advantage of keeping the light source concealed. (See page 67.) If a more even wash of light is required all the way down the wall, then the light needs to be brought away from the wall. A recessed directional downlight or surface-mounted wall washer is the solution, the most discreet option being a low-voltage directional downlight well recessed to prevent glare and with a frosted lens to soften the scallop of light. Another form of emphasis on a textured wall would be to have a series of uplights close to it, grazing up the surface. (See page 30.)

When it comes to stairs, recessing downlights into a sloping soffit is never an ideal option, as the light is always angled in the wrong direction and creates glare. A low-level floor washer, used on each or every other stair tread, depending on the style and wattage, is always a better solution. This is practical, particularly on a narrow staircase that would otherwise be difficult to light. If the staircase is glass, uplighting it from below can provide

> "The idea is to add interest and create contrast, drawing attention to areas that are not usually lit during the day or are lit only by soft background lighting."

OPPOSITE This spiral staircase in a stone turret poses problems to light. It is too narrow for wall lights and the windows are tiny. The ideal solution was to use these recessed floor washers that I designed to be asymmetric with their light source shielded. That way, there is no glare as you ascend the stairs. Used on every third step, the light brings out the texture of the stone and creates a wonderful play of light and shade.

LEFT This column is lit using fiber optics at the base, with a lens used to create a narrow 10-deg. beam of light that accentuates the texture of the column. It is important that the fiber source of light is set well down in its housing to reduce glare—this also means that the light source remains cool because the light box is remote.

some interesting effects, making it a piece of sculpture within the space and providing an effective glow of light on each tread. (See page 145).

The underside of a staircase is often forgotten and can be an area of darkness. Lighting it will have the effect of bringing this potentially dead space into the room or hall, increasing the sense of width and space. Various solutions are possible, such as small recessed uplights close to the back wall to light the underside of the stairs, or a slot at the back to introduce a linear effect of light to accentuate the area otherwise left in shadow. (See page 58.)

In a traditional house, the key features to light, other than the staircase, are the door trim, the fireplace, an arched opening, or a column. The most useful tool in these cases is a low-glare narrow-beam uplight, which should have a spread of no more than 10 degrees, and be positioned in the floor with the lamp (bulb) set well down into the fixture to avoid glare. This should be as close to the feature as possible to create an uplight effect that accentuates each horizontal element, creating a pattern of light and shade. This technique is particularly effective on fire surrounds, adding emphasis to the fireplace when the fire itself is not in use. (See page 38.) Usually a low-voltage halogen source is used, and an LED warm white uplight is an alternative source.

> "When choosing a light source, never be afraid to conduct a lighting test with a sample to ensure that it achieves the effect you require, as this avoids expensive disappointment."

Top tips

Uplighting is often the best way of highlighting an architectural feature, as it brings out the unexpected, highlighting the elements that are not accentuated by natural light during the day and adding interest and contrast. (See page 22.) For example, placing an uplight on either side of fireplace makes it come alive, even when the fire is not lit. (See page 38.)

When using light to focus on a feature—whether an architectural element, a piece of art, or an interesting surface—make sure that it is controlled separately from the other lighting in the room. This allows the general lighting to be lowered to create greater contrast, which in turn makes the feature lighting more prominent. (See pages 22 and 29.)

When an uplight or a downlight is positioned close to a surface—as it needs to be in order to draw attention to a particular feature—the light will also highlight and accentuate the texture. A rough texture will appear more rugged, while a smooth surface (unless it is completely flawless) will have all of its imperfections shown up. (See pages 30–31.)

Even the forgotten areas in a house, such as under the stairs, can become a feature when they are illuminated. This can even help to increase the feeling of space. The dead area under a staircase can be lit with uplights or a continuous slot to bring an appealing new dimension to a hall. (See page 58.) Lighting any niches or recesses will also add interest to the space.

ABOVE In this indoor swimming pool, there is little light except for the lighting within the pool and the low-level floor washers between the arched windows. The windows are lit on each side with recessed uplights that graze up the sides and emphasize the curved stone arches, creating a glow similar to wall lights. Low-voltage 20W 12V light sources were used so that, when dimmed, they could provide a soft glow similar to candlelight. The effect is made even more magical by the wonderful reflections in the pool, doubling the impact of the arches.

These louvers form a moving wall separating a bedroom and bathroom. When the louvers are open, the end blade of each one is lit by the narrow-beam fibers; when the louvers are closed, the lights create a soft scallop effect on the timber wall. The use of fiber-optic lights means that there is no heat at each uplight, and a lens was used to focus the light upward. A small low-voltage downlight with a frosted lens gives a wide wash of light on the shade and onto the chair. Through the louvers, the effect of a narrow-beam downlight can be seen on the stone bathtub.

RIGHT The wonderful carved screen has been lit with a directional low-glare 35W 12V downlight with a medium-beam lamp and a softening lens, which creates a soft arc of light over the screen and throws a shadow below.

BELOW The bronze sculpture by Harry Bertoia near the foot of the stairs is just glanced at by a recessed directional downlight, leaving some of it in shadow. By contrast, the painting by Fritz Bultman has been lit in its entirety with a framing projector. This has a metal mask cut by a specialist into the exact shape of the picture, which makes it appear to be lit from within. The source is a tiny aperture in the ceiling, which is almost invisible. This requires access from above for maintenance.

lighting features and displays

The addition of shelving in the home to display treasured objects or a collection of books or photographs is a fantastic way of creating a feature and focus. With effective lighting, simple shelving can be elevated to an elegant storage unit to create impact in any room. Lit shelves add another layer of light to a space, which is softer and more effective than another downlight.

Glass shelves, especially when used for displaying glass accessories, can be lit through all the layers with low-voltage or LED downlights. Glass is a fantastic medium to illuminate, as it can both absorb and refract light. (See page 37.) Frosted glass contains the light, giving the impression of being lit from within and creating tremendous impact, while clear glass shelves glow green at the edges. In some instances, a glass shelf can be edge-lit using fiber optics or LEDs. Make sure the front edge of the light is frosted, so that you do not see the light source directly. (See page 49.)

Individual shelves can be lit in a number of ways. Simple low-voltage semirecessed undercabinet lights with a small lip to reduce glare can be built into the joinery and used on each shelf to highlight the shelf and objects below. A miniature surface-mounted light is ideal for highlighting individual objects, particularly glass, as unusual shadows are created on the back wall. (See page 62.) Linear shelf lights are useful tools to frontlight or backlight shelves, the latter throwing the objects into silhouette. Lighting can also be fully integrated into the center of the shelving, providing both up and downlight from the shelf.

When lighting bookshelves, the book backs can be simply washed with low-voltage low-glare directional downlights. If recessing is not possible, use a flexible picture light. For dramatic impact, you could backlight the unit with colored light or use wall-mounted lights. (See page 76.)

TOP LEFT This display of plates was a challenge to light—downlights would have created unwanted shadows. A small specially developed light fixture, with a 10W 12V capsule lamp in a customized reflector, was recessed into each corbel to uplight the plates individually. A small LED strip in a reflector could also have been used.

TOP CENTER A 3D metal sculpture is lit with a recessed directional 35W 12V low-voltage downlight that catches the surface and provides a double image with the unusual shadows cast on the wall behind.

TOP RIGHT Backlit shelves throw the objects displayed on them into silhouette and give the room a soft infill light. The shelves are spaced 2-in. (50mm) from the wall, and the strip light is placed behind. Depending on the effect required, various light sources can be used—a 240V rope light for a soft glow, a xenon clickstrip for a brighter tungsten halogen source that can be dimmed, a slimline fluorescent for a cool effect, or an LED strip behind a frosted diffuser.

ABOVE LEFT For sculptures acquired after the lighting has been planned, such as this one by Harry Bertoia, plug-in solutions are ideal. A 20W 12V low-glare spotlight is mounted on a column that houses the transformer. Light catches some of the panels, making patterns on the wall.

ABOVE RIGHT The drawing by David Hockney, *Interior with a Lamp,* is lit with a framing projector, which works in the same ways as described for the picture opposite. The shelves are frontlit using a tungsten clickstrip, which gives a very soft, warm light. Another possible source is a warm white LED, although the color is not as good. Its advantages are its compact size, long lamp life, and lower energy consumption.

RIGHT This silk wallpaper has a wonderful texture and has been dramatically lit using recessed low-voltage uplights with narrow-beam 12-deg. lamps positioned close to the wall. The effect exaggerates the texture, because the light catches every projecting silk knot in the weave and casts shadows above. A similar effect can be achieved on any surface using close offset lighting, but care must be taken when lighting a plain, flat-plastered wall or a drywall in this way, as any imperfections will also be highlighted.

OPPOSITE TOP The old chimneypiece in this bathroom is lit by a variety of lighting effects. Three small downlights located within the chimney breast send light down the wall and accentuate the pattern of the brickwork. The ceramic vase on the mantel is backlit, and a narrow spotlight highlights its smooth surface, in contrast to the rugged texture of the fireplace. The spotlight illuminating the curved chimney breast is on a beam above and uses a medium-beam lamp. This produces an even wash of light that results in a far smoother effect on the same rough brickwork.

OPPOSITE BOTTOM These textured timber doors respond well to the soft wall wash of light, which emphasizes the deep grain pattern of the wood that seems almost flat when seen in daylight. Individual fixtures light each pair of doors using wide-beam 40-deg. lamps and frosted lenses. A wall wash on cupboard doors is a useful way of bringing additional general light into a room.

Decorate surfaces

The way light hits a surface can create different effects and change the way you see that surface. Depending on the result you wish to achieve, light can be used to enhance the surface by highlighting its color or texture. It can create patterns on It by reflection or refraction, or it can project color.

creating texture

The texture of a wall or floor can be smooth, rough, soft, shiny, or matte. The way to interpret this is entirely dependent on the way it is lit. For example, if light is projected toward a rough wall from a distance, then the light will wash over the wall, producing a much smoother effect. The wall will appear to be flatter and less rugged, as the shadows will be reduced. Moving the light source closer to the wall, so that the light hits the surface at a more oblique angle, will increase the texture. This is because the areas that are lit and the shadows these create become more pronounced. So, if you wish to make a surface appear more textured, close offset lighting will provide a more dramatic effect. The opposite, of course, is true—providing a soft, even wash of light at a distance will keep the surface looking very flat and smooth.

Be aware that any close offset lighting will also highlight any imperfections, as light can be very unforgiving and any undulations in a surface will be thrown into relief. This is particularly important when considering external lighting because what looks like perfect brickwork by daylight can appear rough when lit at night. Be careful when lighting tile for the same reason: lights positioned to skim down the back wall of a shower will draw attention to any uneven tiling. This is especially true of mosaic tiles, which are better lit by a softer, flatter light.

Light will also bring out the different qualities of matte and shiny surfaces. A wool blanket, for example, will absorb the light and appear soft and flat, whereas satin or silk will reflect light, which makes its surface shine and bounce light back into the room.

color

Colored light creates the most dramatic effect in a white space, because white walls will strongly reflect the color projected against it. A colored wall will take on the hue of the light, but will not reflect it in the same way. Any objects in the space will also reflect the color.

Often seen in bars and restaurants, colored light can be used within the home as a fun feature in a home theater or child's room, to introduce an accent color, or perhaps to backlight a glass panel in a bathroom. Color can also be used with glass to create a changing and dramatic effect. A glass screen with a frosted pattern can be edge-lit, so that light travels through the clear glass, and color will show only where the frosted elements are. The screen can be white or changed at the touch of a button to shocking pink or midnight blue.

The most popular source is LEDs (light-emitting diodes), which are made up of the primary colors of light: red, green, and blue. Combining these creates white light, but an infinite palette of colors can be achieved by changing the balance of the three colors. A more straightforward method, producing a subtle effect, is to use a gel over a light source.

ABOVE The color in this apartment is simply created by using two white light sources of different color temperatures, one of 2,400K (warm) and one of about 5,000K (cool). Seen together, their individual effect seems to be exaggerated by the contrast. The shelves are lit with a linear tungsten halogen source (which is filament-based) made of lots of miniature lamps on a linear metal track, often called "clickstrip." When dimmed it provides a soft, warm, inviting glow and is the main source of light within the space at night. In the center is a glass staircase leading to the glass-floor mezzanine level. This is internally lit for a sculptural effect, using cool white LED strips. It appears almost as an ice block within the space.

RIGHT The colored light on this staircase changes the mood and decorates an otherwise white space. The frosted-glass stairs have been uplit using RGB (red, green, blue) LEDs. Together, they make white light, but by controlling the red, green, and blue light elements individually in different proportions it is possible to achieve almost any color combination.

OPPOSITE Another view of the same stairs, now in blue. The saturation of the color is intensified by the white walls, but the effect is subtle, rather than overpowering.

Color temperatures

Light sources have different "color temperatures," making some appear whiter than others. Use color sparingly for fun and impact, but play with the qualities of white light, and use it to create different effects within the home.

Fluorescents, with a color temperature of 5,000K, give an icy white light, which can be too harsh and clinical. The best way to use these energy-efficient lights for a daylight effect is either diffused behind glass or bounced off the ceiling.

Incandescent lamps create light by heating up the internal filament to such a high temperature that both light and heat are produced. The resulting light has a color temperature of about 2,700K and a warmer appearance.

Manufacturers found that halogen gas inserted in the glass casing of an incandescent lamp created a whiter light with a color temperature of 300K. When the aim is to achieve the feeling of sun streaming into an interior, a halogen lamp does the job.

A room that is decorated in a warm color such as beige or red will be enhanced by a warmer light source, whereas a blue or green room will be accentuated by a cooler white light because there is more blue light in its color spectrum.

pattern | Thinking of light in terms of pattern may seem strange. Pattern is usually achieved with wallpaper, carpet, or other materials. In terms of light, incredible patterned effects can be created through a play of light and shadow, and unlike a pattern on a material, this changes as the light moves and disappears entirely when the light is off. When light is projected onto an object, it lights the object, but projects the image of its outline in reverse on the surface below. (See page 36.) Moving the angle of the light or the object will change the effect of the pattern. The more oblique the angle of the light, the more abstract the pattern will become. Pattern can also be created by backlighting an object such as a piece of fretwork or a carved screen. Displayed on a wall, the pattern may be barely revealed, but a light between the two surfaces will add a different dimension.

One of the most familiar ways of achieving pattern through light is with a Moroccan lantern—or any perforated light shade. This creates wonderful patterns of light and shadow on the surrounding walls and ceiling. The shadow created will be sharper when a clear incandescent lamp (bulb) is used rather than a pearl or frosted lamp, which projects a softer-edged image. Another way of creating pattern with light is to use the point source itself, which could be arranged as a matrix, in a random pattern (such as stars in a ceiling), or in any other formation.

OPPOSITE LEFT In this steam room, it is as though an array of stars twinkles among the tiled mosaic. The main light source is the downlight providing the soft pool of light. The stars are created using tiny fiber-optic tails incorporated into the mosaic ceiling; then cut flush with the tiling. When they are on, they create a starlight effect that can be made to flicker if required. The light source is remote (ideal when used in a steam room), and the light travels down the fibers from the light box and emits at the ends. A color wheel or flicker wheel makes the fibers twinkle like stars. A low-voltage halogen source is usually used for small installations. For larger installations, a metal halide source, which has more power, may be used, but this light source takes a while to warm up and does not dim.

OPPOSITE RIGHT This Moroccan mirror with a Jali screen frame is lit from behind, putting the frame into silhouette and creating a soft light. Reflected in the mirror is a decorative Jali screen, which is also backlit so that the pattern is seen in silhouette. The source is xenon clickstrip, chosen for its warm color. Other options are a sleeved fluorescent for a colored effect or a linear LED strip.

ABOVE LEFT The pattern on the wooden screen is highlighted with a soft downlight, emphasizing the mother-of-pearl detail. The stars are projected using fiber optics, from a small aperture in the ceiling with a mask in the shape of a star.

ABOVE RIGHT In this Moroccan-themed guest bathroom, a simple fretwork mask has been placed around a recessed downlight on the ceiling, throwing the pattern of the fretwork into silhouette. The pattern around the light comes from the reflections off the polished stainless-steel sink below (out of view). At the side, the Moroccan-style wall light casts patterns against the wall. To achieve the sharpest patterns from a perforated lantern, use a clear incandescent lamp: a pearl lamp will not create the same sharp shadows.

Create contrast
The key to successful and creative lighting is understanding how to manipulate what is lit and what is left in shadow so that you can achieve the most dynamic effects.

ABOVE The vase of flowers on the glass coffee table are dramatically lit with a single downlight that catches the flowers and projects a sharp shadow of their shape onto the floor below. If two lights had been used, the shadows would have been softer and less in focus.

RIGHT Recessed uplights have been positioned at intervals close to the wall to create narrow shafts of light that graze up the wall's surface, forming pools of light on the ceiling and reflecting back softly. Special 20W 12V low-heat uplights have been used, with the lamp set well down in the fixture—by about 3 in. (75mm)—thus causing little glare to diners at the table. The significant contrast between the lit and unlit sections of the wall creates a dramatic dynamic.

light, shadow, and silhouette

When we "see," light reflects off an object and gives us a visual impression of that object. The amount and manner of reflection depend on the surface that is being lit—a dark matte surface reflects far less light than a bright white surface, for example. Our understanding of an object is therefore determined by how light reflects off it.

Depending on the angle from which it is lit, a three-dimensional object will have different amounts of light striking it on all sides—one side may be strongly lit, while the other is less so and can be described as being in shadow. It is the combination of light and shade that lets us interpret three-dimensional objects— the shadow is as important as the part that is lit, telling us the full story.

Any scene that is created by a combination of light and shadow is far more interesting than one that is lit uniformly. This is true of daylight as well—think of the dramatic shadow cast when the sun strikes a building compared to the same building seen under a cloudy sky. Look through holiday photographs and see how a scene that looks flat and dull on an overcast day takes on new life and interest when the sun is shining.

Top tips

If an object has an unusual shape, lighting it from behind to throw it into silhouette will accentuate this and have more impact than lighting it from the front. Often a recessed or plug-in uplight positioned behind the object can be enough to create the magic.

A sculpture may be more effectively lit from one side, as the sculpture tells a better story when part of it is left in shadow. If it is lit from both sides,

there will be no shadows, and the effect will be less dramatic. The trick is to choose which side of the sculpture to light to achieve the best effect.

An object that is lit from above will create dramatic shadows on the surface below. If the object is lit with a single light source, the resulting shadow will be sharp and defined, while two light sources cross-lighting the object will cast shadows with softer edges.

BELOW The bold architraves of this doorway were created with columns of square glass shelves, which contrast with the dark wood surrounds. They are made more impressive when lit from the top and bottom by 20W 12V up-and-downlights. The glass shelves are frosted with clear centers, so the light passes through the middle and illuminates the frosted sections.

To create an exciting and dynamic lighting scheme, it is essential to understand how to achieve a successful balance of what is lit and what remains unlit. Don't be afraid of shadow, but instead have fun manipulating light and playing with how an object is lit to create different effects with silhouette and shadow. A dark object, such as a bronze sculpture, can be lit dramatically from behind so that its outline is revealed in silhouette, while adding some frontlighting will fill out and highlight more of the detail and form. In the same way, lighting a carved screen from behind reveals its pattern in a totally different way than when it is frontlit and the detail of the carving is highlighted. Sending light through such a screen reveals its pattern on the neighboring surface; if the angle of the light is oblique, then the pattern will be distorted and abstract. (See pages 34 and 35.)

ABOVE LEFT Two uplights define each side of a minimalist fireplace, while at the same time highlighting the 3D blocks above—*No. 109* by Sophie Smallhorn. The light provides a playful game of light and shadow, which is enhanced by the flickering of the fire. The light sources are 20W 12V medium-beam halogen lamps, which are concealed behind the two timber blocks.

ABOVE RIGHT This classical fire surround is lit from the bottom at either side in the same way as the minimalist fireplace shown on the left,

but with two bronze low-voltage uplights. It is important to choose a fixture where the lamp is set well back to avoid glare. The sculptural contours of the fireplace are defined and thrown into relief by the areas of light and shadow, a technique that ensures the fireplace remains a focus even when the fire is not lit. The bronze sculpture on the mantelpiece by Patricia Udell is grazed with soft indirect light, while the sculpture on the side table by Kim James is lit from above by a task light to one side, creating focus.

OPPOSITE This entrance hall shows how different layers of light create an interesting overall effect. The unusual wall lights with their metal shades send light up and down, bathing the timber bench. A small spotlight, with a remote transformer located on the beam above, is focused on the central picture. The uneven texture of the old tiled floor is emphasized by floor washers recessed in the wall, which direct light to the floor on either side and underneath the bench. The combination of effects builds up the scene, each one being equally important.

Set the mood

Understanding the effects that can be achieved with light allows us to create visual impact within a room, which can be altered throughout the day as natural light levels change. A flexible scheme, where both the focus and light levels can be adjusted, is key.

BELOW AND OPPOSITE The same living room lit under different conditions shows the power of light in creating mood. When light is provided by only low-voltage halogen lights (below), it is whiter, cooler, and sharper. This would be used as a supplement to natural daylight, when a crisper, whiter light is more compatible. On a dull day, this setting will make the room feel as though sunlight is streaming into it. The lamps and shelf lighting are off, as their color is too warm for daytime. When the room is lit for evening (opposite), the general light is dimmed to a warm, inviting glow and the cupboards are less bright. The focus changes to the center of the room, and the soft lighting of the shelves and wall lights comes into play. This sets the mood for entertaining. The painting by Kurt Jackson above the fireplace is lit with a low-glare downlight.

changing the ambiance of a room with lighting

It is necessary to understand the effects of light in order to set the mood of a room and create visual impact within a space that can change from day to evening. In a well-planned scheme, the various lighting effects are built up in layers, so that the room can be lit in different ways to create different moods, depending on the level and quality of light required at any given time. The key is not to use all the effects simultaneously or to the same intensity. Each light effect should be controlled separately so that they can be combined at different levels and brought up individually to alter the ambiance in the room.

"To create atmosphere, the key is not to use all the light effects simultaneously or to the same intensity, but to bring them up individually as required."

LEFT A soft, inviting mood has been created in this space by the warm tungsten light of the double-height bookshelves and the table lamp. When the central glass staircase is lit from within with white LEDs, it introduces an icy white light. (See page 32.) In the evening, the contrast between the two color temperatures can be too much; keeping all the light sources the same can lead to a softer, more relaxing mood. The sculpture in front of the bookshelves is *Yoko X (sitting)* by Don Brown.

OPPOSITE LEFT AND RIGHT The feel and atmosphere of a simple corridor changes entirely when it is lit with contrasting lighting effects. On the left, downlights used to light the floor slightly catch the walls. The last downlight, directed with a soft 40-deg. lamp and frosted lens, provides focus on the shade at the end. This is the background effect to use during the day. By contrast, at night low-level lights create a more dramatic effect. These are set into the walls above the baseboard and are used to light the floor. A combination of the two effects could be used in the early evening, going to a dimmed version of just the low-level floor washers late at night.

During the day, natural light is often sufficient, but on dull and overcast days, introducing artificial lighting can give a room a welcome "lift." You could usually achieve this by bringing up the general lighting rather than the effects, which can be kept for creating mood settings later in the day. In a kitchen, for example, the general lighting may be recessed downlights lighting the fronts of cupboards, uplighting providing a wash of light on the ceiling, or the focused light over a kitchen table. At this stage, you would not necessarily bring out any display lighting or low-level lighting below kitchen cupboards, as these would not be seen with full impact during the day and would be a waste of energy.

As daylight fades, the necessity for more lighting increases. At dusk, when there is still some daylight outside, you almost need to increase the light level inside because you want to maintain a feeling of brightness for as long as possible. This all changes when it is dark outside, and the warmth of a soft, moody atmosphere becomes far more desirable, and you can get away with less light. The general lights can then be dimmed, and the effect lighting—such as low-level lighting under a kitchen island, localized undercabinet task light, and any display lighting—introduced. The mood of a room is altered by the change of emphasis—the softening of light by dimming, which makes its color warmer, and introducing highlights to different areas, making them appear totally different than in daylight. Examples include lighting shelves, backlighting a niche or uplighting an architectural detail. Light gives you the power to

change the focus—daylight is always the dominant source and lights everything in its path, but at night you can emphasize areas that were left in shadow during the day.

One of the key ways to change the mood is by using dimmers to create a softer, warmer feel as the color temperature of the light source is reduced. This is easy to do with conventional (incandescent) sources—such as the standard bulb in a table lamp or with low-voltage halogen lamps—but it is harder to achieve with other light sources, because the way they are made does not allow their color temperature to change when they are dimmed; they just reduce in output. Both fluorescent and LED sources fall into this category—they can be dimmed, becoming less bright, but their color does not change, which can make them seem flat and almost gray. In order to include an energy-efficient fluorescent source (which is primarily used for general lighting) within a scheme, the solution may be to have two light sources—a cooler one for use in the day and a warmer one (maybe even filtered) that can be dimmed at night. This is possible if the light source is concealed, such as in an uplight in a cove or above joinery where two sources could be combined, or in a custom pendant in which they can be integrated from the outset.

"Change the mood by changing the direction of the light—an uplight has a very different effect to a downlight, and using the two selectively can have powerful results."

ABOVE AND OPPOSITE A wall of glass on one side of this penthouse apartment's living room means that the entire space is bathed in natural light during the day. In the evening and on cloudy days, the atmosphere is governed by the lighting, which is built up of many discreet elements that can be controlled individually to set the mood. Lamps provide general light and a visual focus. The lit shelves highlight objects and provide a similar soft infill light to the lamp light. The dramatic glass architrave surrounding the doors and framing the entrance to the master suite adds interest and contrasts with the dark wood shelves. (See page 37.) In front of them is a slot in the ceiling with a skylight above, through which natural light floods in during the day. At night, it is lit with miniature capsule lamps, creating a glow and reflecting off the glass. This provides a soft high-level light, similar to a dimmed chandelier or pendant. (See page 95.) Four low-glare recessed downlights with 10-deg. lamps create a central

focus on the coffee table in the area where people gather. The mood is altered by controlling each of these elements separately and setting them to different levels. In the first image, all the light sources are brighter and whiter; by dimming them as in the second picture, the warmth of the light is increased, creating a softer, more intimate space.

"Always fit dimmers so that you can change the mood of a room. Having more than one circuit, each controlled by a dimmer, allows you to create a variety of lighting effects."

Add drama

It is the contrast between light and shadow that brings a sense of drama to a space. This may be an elaborate scheme that dominates a long corridor or walkway, or decorates an entire wall, or a simple device such as a spotlight focused on a single object.

RIGHT This is the theatrical view of a water feature leading down from a pavilion. The contrast between the surrounding darkness and the lit pavilion sets the tone. The pavilion is lit with two main light sources. Downlights located behind the columns softly light the facade, while the columns themselves are lit in front with recessed uplights, a pair to each column. The water runs down in steps, with each fall of water being lit with three underwater LED lights.

OPPOSITE This atmospheric guest bathroom is almost entirely illuminated by the alabaster sink, which is lit internally by a fluorescent source that is diffused to a warm glow. The only other source is a downlight that lights the dark polished plaster wall and catches the orchid sitting on top of the sink.

theatrical lighting and dramatic effects

Dramatic effects are created when there is a significant contrast between light and dark. It is the interplay between the two that is visually arresting and creates the drama in a space. Creating drama relies on lighting controls and the ability to set levels of light individually to maximize contrast and achieve theatrical effects. A technique as simple as dimming all other light sources except, perhaps, a single downlight focused on a vase of flowers can be sufficient. A corridor, for example, lit with a row of downlights with wide-beam lamps, will appear entirely different when narrow-beam lamps are used in those same downlights, creating pools or stepping stones of light through areas of shadow.

One thing to think about when selecting the most appropriate general light as a backdrop to a dramatic effect is that reflected or diffused light often provides softer background lighting than a direct downlighting source. Reflected light is achieved when light is bounced off walls as a wall-wash effect or off the ceiling as an uplight effect.

ABOVE Narrow beams of light always create drama, partly because of the contrast between what is lit and what remains in darkness. This entrance is framed by two recessed uplights. Inside, narrow pools of light focus on the floor of the conservatory. As there is no fixed roof, these pools are created by 50W 12V spots on a wire track. Along the back wall is a series of brick piers, each of which is lit by an up-and-downlight using two 20W 12V narrow-beam lamps, dramatically emphasizing their texture.

RIGHT Narrow shafts of light from low-glare low-heat 20W 12V uplights create a playful pattern like columns of light along the wall.

OPPOSITE This small bar area is made both dramatic and glamorous by the play between the lacquered deep violet backdrop and the transparency of the glass. There are two main lighting effects working together. The first is the simple low-voltage downlight that casts light through the shelves, highlighting the objects in its path and creating a pool of light on the glass countertop. In addition, there is a slimline fluorescent edge-lighting each of the glass shelves and making them appear to float.

LEFT This unusual stone sink incorporates fiber-optic lights in the spout and set into the basin, which light up as the water flows. There is no faucet; when you place your hands under the spout, the water starts to flow and seems to be internally lit. This is an effect used by many contemporary shower manufacturers to combine the decorative effects of light and water.

RIGHT The drama of this dining room is created by the effect of layering light and controlling each element separately. The centerpiece is the chandelier, which uses halogen uplights that throw patterns through its structure across the ceiling. Around the chandelier are four low-glare 35W 12V downlights with honeycomb louvers that reduce glare. These focus a soft light onto the table, which is ideal for dining. To the left, a rugged stone wall is wall-washed, providing a soft reflected light. The view through the floor-to-ceiling window is of the city beyond. The trick preventing the window from creating reflections of the room is to light something immediately beyond it. In this case, a row of small uplights has been positioned on the terrace outside to illuminate the slatted-timber trellis.

Top tips

Drama is created by contrast, so try to be selective—lighting a single key item in a space and leaving the rest in shadow can be more dramatic than lighting every feature.

When assessing how to light a space, think of ways to bring out a sense of theater—for instance, creating an avenue of uplights in a hall, leading to a single downlight focusing on a feature at the end, will produce dramatic results because of the contrast between the effects.

Stunning visual effects can be achieved through a play of light and shade. Lighting through an open trellis, blind, or screen can result in dramatic shadows.

Ensure that the general lighting is controlled separately to the feature lighting, as there are times—especially during the day—when you will only want to use the former. At night, the background lighting should be dimmed down to a low level so that the feature lighting becomes the key player.

Remember the dramatic potential of exterior lighting. At night, make the most of lit areas outside your window. By keeping the interior lighting low, the eye travels to the brighter feature lights outside, whether in a garden or on a roof terrace. If the interior lighting is too bright, it will create reflections in the glass and prevent you from seeing and enjoying any of the effects outside. It is important to have a lit feature immediately beyond the window to draw the eye.

LIGHTING AT WORK

The wide range of light effects that can be achieved means that lighting can be employed within the home in many different ways. Soft, diffuse background lighting fills a room with the general light that we see by, in contrast to dramatic accent lighting that creates points of focus and direct task lighting that is required for purely practical purposes. Discreet concealed lighting can be used in diverse ways to accentuate architecture and highlight features, while decorative light adds interest and creates a visual reference.

Background lighting Also

known as general light or ambient light, background light is the practical overall lighting within a room. This can be achieved by various means, and the best solution depends on the room in question.

When deciding on the most appropriate solution for a room's background lighting, think about its main uses and the tasks that will be performed there; then decide how best to achieve the general light. In a living space, for example, the background light may be provided by a chandelier, lamps, and wall lights; in a utility room, it could be uplighting or downlighting, or a combination of these. Various effects can be achieved when chandeliers or decorative lamps are used as the general light. For example, a chandelier with exposed lamps (bulbs) will create a totally different effect from one with diffusing shades.

If using recessed lights to achieve background light in a kitchen, bathroom, or hallway, try to arrange them so that they relate to the layout of the space and are not necessarily laid out in a grid formation. While the latter will give totally even illumination, this can make a space feel more like an office than a home. In addition, most people hate to stand or walk directly under a light, as it can cast an uncomfortable shadow. A better solution is to create some reflected light by directing these downlights toward the walls or cabinets so that the light reflects off the surface. This "wall washing" will result in a far softer effect.

When using recessed lights for general light in this way, bear in mind that their effect will be strongly governed by whatever they are lighting. If the walls or floor are dark, then the reflected light will be significantly reduced. If the ceiling is the only light color in the room, then uplight this. It is important to recognize that the color and reflection of the walls in an interior play an important part in how light is affected. In a totally white space, the reflection is at its greatest, and the amount of light required to make the room seem bright will be comparatively less than in a dark

(continued on page 59)

> **"Think of background lighting as you would the main paint color in a room—the basis from which an interior designer plays with layers to build up the overall effect, and the starting point from which all other accents, tones, and textures spring."**

The general light in this kitchen is created by the strip lights above the top row of cabinets, which give a soft indirect light. This is supplemented by the small low-glare, low-voltage downlights, which provide task lighting for the countertops, and highlight the stainless-steel finishes. The focus over the central island is the high-tech pendant incorporating a grid of four directional downlights.

BELOW Various lighting effects are at work in this traditional kitchen. Strip lights above the tall cabinets throw the urns into silhouette. The light source could be either low-voltage xenon, which provides a white light that can be dimmed at night, or a combination of fluorescent for day and a soft, warm rope light to provide the background light at night as part of the dining setting. In addition, the chandelier over the table gives useful general light, with a cleverly concealed downlight in its base that highlights the plate of oranges. Six pendants provide working light for the kitchen island.

OPPOSITE The background light in this dressing room is the soft, indirect uplight from a continuous track of low-voltage xenon lights on top of the built-in closet (a warm white LED strip would create a similar effect). The light is reflected off the white walls and ceiling, and bounced back into the room. The effect of the downlights in the ceiling would be harsher and less interesting without this. A contemporary chandelier has been used over the central drawer unit to create a visual focus. At first glance, this appears to be the main light source in the room.

Top tips

The level of background light depends on the predominant color scheme of the room, as well as the light sources chosen and the number of fixtures used.

Decorative light fixtures are usually used only to provide the background light in areas that can get away with relatively low levels of general light, such as living rooms, bedrooms, and dining rooms. In such areas, the other effects of accent and task lighting will boost the light levels and provide the impact.

Uplighting is a particularly effective way to use low-energy sources for background lighting because the effect is softened by reflection off the ceiling.

LEFT The area under the stairs is often forgotten and falls into shadow, but lighting it can increase the feeling of space. Here, a line of xenon or an LED tape light could be used as the source. Concealed by a small cornice or beam, and fitted to the underside of the stairs approximately 4 in. (100mm) from the wall, these provide a soft wall-wash effect. A fluorescent light source would appear too harsh in the home, and if dimmed, the color would be too gray.

OPPOSITE The general light in this library is created by the same light source—a line of xenon or an LED tape light—fitted into the underside of the chunky bookshelves, making them appear as though they are floating.

wood or painted room in which light is absorbed and little is reflected. A simple way to test this theory is to hold a piece of white cardstock under a downlight, then a black or dark-colored cardstock, and observe the difference in reflection on the ceiling.

Uplight is a form of background light that is much softer than direct downlight. This can be from a freestanding floor uplight, a wall-mounted uplight, or a linear fitting concealed above a cove in the ceiling or above cabinets. It provides an excellent basis for general light because it is soft and diffuse, with few sharp shadows so that any accent light punched through it immediately creates contrast. The same rules apply: a white ceiling offers the best reflectance, but a matte surface is preferable to a shiny one. A shiny surface will reflect the light source itself, which will look unsightly, and the even wash, described above, will not be achieved.

"The level of general light will always be greater in a white or pale-colored room than in a room decorated in dark hues, as pale surfaces reflect more light than dark ones, which absorb it."

Accent lighting

This is where the fun with lighting is to be had. Once you have achieved an overall level of background light appropriate for the room in question, lighting the space in a general way, it is the accent lighting that creates the interest and focus and creates the contrast within the room.

Introducing accent lighting allows you to play with some dramatic effects, such as defining features and creating contrast. Each effect helps to build up the scene and create the mood, and should be controlled separately from the other light effects in the room. Accent lighting may be a picture light over a painting, a narrow beam of light focused on a vase of flowers, a backlight behind a sculpture, or an uplight highlighting an architectural detail such as an arch or fireplace.

When planning the accent lighting for a room, first decide on the main features to be lit, and create a hierarchy. For example, if every picture on a wall is lit by a row of downlights, the effect will be more of a wall wash and becomes general background light, rather than creating a specific highlight. As a general rule, if you add too much accent lighting, the impact will be lost, so it is important to be selective and light only key pieces. If there are three pictures above a sofa with lamps on either side, for instance, instead of lighting all three pictures with recessed ceiling lights, it may be more effective to focus on the central one and rely on the uplight from the lamps to light the others. Deciding on what is lit, and what is not, is crucial because achieving a good balance is what creates the harmony in a room.

RIGHT In this bathroom, a marble slab has been used as a wall to separate the bathtub from the shower. The downlights located within the shower area give the marble a wonderful backlit translucent quality. This, together with the lit niche above the bathtub, helps to provide the mood lighting on the lower settings. The niche is lit with a sealed low-voltage source with a frosted lens to create a softer, wider beam of light.

FAR RIGHT A central courtyard forms the focus of this space. The narrow-beam uplights, shining against the polished plaster wall at the back of the picture, are particularly effective at emphasizing the horizontal banding—light always hits and accentuates any horizontals in its path. The courtyard trees are uplit with two 20W 12V medium-beam uplights set low within the planters. The floor seems to be aglow with the dance of night-lights. These are, in fact, small bubble jets internally illuminated by fiber optics. When neither the water nor fibers are lit, the courtyard seems flat and uninteresting, but at the touch of a switch both the water and light come into action to create a dynamic display, which is given added drama by the reflections in the glazing.

"Do not light every object or picture in a room, but be selective and decide at the outset which are going to be the main, real points. Too much accent light will lessen the impact, and the light will become general background light, rather than highlighting a particular feature."

ABOVE Shelf units provide an interesting focal point in this living room. The decorative wall lights define the "look." Small 10W 12V footlights are used in some of the niches to light objects, whereas the niches with books are simply wall-washed from the ceiling. Controlling the effects separately allows greater contrast to be created with accent lights.

RIGHT The dramatic fireplace is the focus of this contemporary living room. The kinetic effect of the fire is very important in setting the mood. The stone panels above are lit with low-voltage downlights, creating interest through the individual shafts of light.

picture lighting

The choice of picture lighting falls into two main categories: wall-mounted and ceiling-mounted. In terms of the former, the best option is a frame-mounted picture light, as this casts light directly onto the picture. Usually the power outlet would be mounted approximately 69 inches (1,750mm) above floor level, or it could be dropped down from an electrified plate rail. Because this type of fixture is close to the picture, a tungsten source is not ideal for lighting heavily glazed oil paintings, or prints and watercolors behind glass, as the source will be reflected; it can also become too hot for some artworks. Newer low-voltage picture lights have an arm that extends more than traditional picture lights and directs the light upward, so a direct reflection of the source is avoided and there is a better spread of light on the painting. A flat transformer should be mounted onto the wall behind the picture. This solution works best in tall rooms because the extended arm will be less noticeable; it should not be used in hallways, where ceiling-mounted downlights are the best option.

Ceiling-mounted picture lights can be either surface-mounted spotlights or recessed halogen spotlights. These work well because they have different beam widths to suit different paintings—narrow for a small painting where extra punch is required and wide for a large painting. In addition, lenses can be added to remove the arcs of light and to soften the effect. Use a frosted lens for a very diffuse, almost wall-wash effect—suitable for tapestries or fabric wall hangings—and a spreader lens to elongate the light on a long, narrow picture. The low-voltage low-glare downlight can offer all sorts of options. In a low-ceilinged room, it should be positioned fairly close to the wall on which the picture is hung, within 14–16 inches (350–400mm); in a room with a high ceiling, it can be 40–47 inches (1,000–1,200mm).

Another fully recessed light source is the framing projector. For best effect, this is fully recessed with a tiny visible aperture. Access for maintenance is required in the floor above, if possible, or by means of a discreet panel in the ceiling. If there is a sound system in the room, a recessed speaker can provide access to the light source. (See also pages 28–29.)

Plug-in solutions can be useful for lighting pictures that have been added at a later date. A small spotlight placed unobtrusively on a table can uplight a picture on the wall behind, while a simple table lamp with the right shade will cast an arc of light upward.

LEFT In traditional homes or those in which the interior decoration is complete, it may be difficult to introduce various effects of accent lighting, such as a recessed spotlight, in the ceiling. In addition, some modern light sources may look too intrusive. Here, a plug-in "Clicktray"—a line of xenon lamps in a customized holder with a rubber backing—has been used. This has been positioned on top of the Chinese chest to backlight the wonderful shapes of the pottery in front of it. The light creates an interesting effect, silhouetting and highlighting the soft curves.

RIGHT The accent light in this living area is created from the pools of light that are stronger than the ambient light. The flowers on the coffee table are brought into focus by a 4-deg. 50W 12V low-glare downlight recessed in the double-height ceiling. The narrow beam means that the light is still focused, even over the 16½ ft (5m) it has to travel. Next to the window, the picture creates another focus, being lit by a small directional 50W 12V downlight using a medium-beam 24-deg. lamp.

Concealed lighting

The key to successful lighting is to not to see the source of light, but just the effect it creates. This effect may be considered part of the background lighting or the accent lighting, and there are various techniques that can be used to conceal the source.

Usually, a light source can be concealed by molding. This is true of lights incorporated into a niche or shelving, or those inserted behind a shelf to create backlight. To provide a wash of light on a wall, a light can be recessed in a slot between the edge of the wall and the ceiling. This effect will always result in a stronger light at the top of the wall and a wash that does not remain even all the way down. Sometimes a light source can be located under a table or shelf to create a floating effect, which can be especially effective in a bathroom as a night-light. This will also provide a wash of light on the floor. When using this technique, however, consider the nature of the surfaces that will be lit. If the floor has a polished finish, for example, the light source will be reflected and the effect ruined.

Concealed lighting does not have to be a continuous source. It could be a downlight positioned under a bench or shelf, or in a slot between the wall and the ceiling providing shafts of light down the wall. When used in a shower, this technique can be doubly useful, as the ventilation fan can also be hidden within the slot.

ABOVE In this shower cubicle, a small 20W 12V downlight with a frosted lens is concealed within the niche and provides accent light on the ammonite. Below the stone bench, two 20W 12V recessed wall lights skim light across the floor. The key technique here is to use narrow-beam lights positioned close to floor level, otherwise the effect will be lost.

LEFT This ornate Moroccan door is framed by a horseshoe arch. The shape of the arch and the intricate detail on the door itself are emphasized by small low-heat 20W 12V uplights. It is important that the lamp is set well down within the fixture, by at least 2 in. (50mm), to reduce glare. The uplight highlights the door's surface and catches the shape of the arch.

OPPOSITE Here a slot close to the wall conceals a fluorescent lighting strip providing a linear wall wash. Similar effects could be achieved with other linear sources. To maximize the effect, it is important that the area around the fitting is painted matte white for optimum reflection.

Concealed lighting ideas

Downlights can be set into the toe-kick area under kitchen cabinets to skim across the floor. A glow of light under a solid mass will make it appear to float.

In a shower, recessed wall lights at low level add drama and are useful as night-lights, while downlights set into a recess create shafts of light down the wall.

A concealed strip of light underneath a floating shelf or behind a built-in bench can add a soft glow of light to a room. (See page 71.)

Lighting the underside of a staircase with a concealed strip of light can highlight an otherwise forgotten area and increase a sense of space. (See page 58.)

A concealed light in an unused fireplace introduces a feature that would otherwise be forgotten and makes it an point of interest. (See page 31.)

RIGHT These two recessed windows dressed with silk shades become features in their own right. In the top of each window recess, two small 20W 12V low-voltage downlights with wide-beam lamps give a soft light down the shades and focus on the plants below. As with any downlight, a fixture in which the lamp is well recessed within its housing to avoid direct glare is essential.

OPPOSITE TOP The unusual detail in this bathroom is the continuous recessed area at chair-rail level all the way around the room. This has been emphasized using a concealed lightstream or rope light, an effect that is not used during the day, but works effectively as an unobtrusive night-light.

BELOW This horizontal niche has been created by a projecting windowsill with an exterior-rated xenon light recessed to provide a continuous effect. The light can either be bright or be dimmed to a very low level, almost creating the effect of a night-light.

RIGHT The nickel-framed mirror has been "floated" away from the wall using a warm fluorescent source (color temperature 2,800K) concealed behind it. This reflects off the rear wall, providing a good diffuse light that is flattering to the face. This effect works well as a means of lighting when there are light-colored side returns off which the light can reflect. Without the side walls, the result would be a halo of light, which is not effective for face lighting.

BELOW RIGHT This niche is lit with a small 20W 12V downlight concealed at the top. It uses a narrow-beam 10-deg. lamp to ensure that the light travels through the thick glass shelves and highlights the vases.

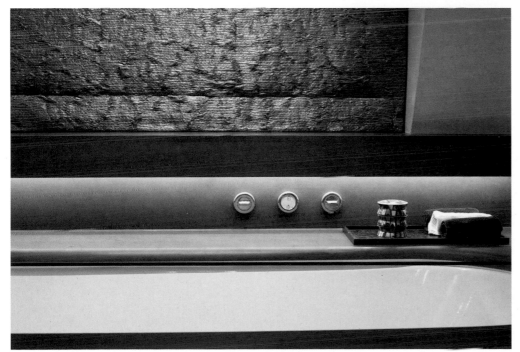

RIGHT The window that is hidden behind this shade is actually half the size of the shade, but its proportion has been improved by the combined effect of the shade and clever lighting. This effect requires two shades—a blackout shade at the back and a translucent shade at the front. At either side of the window, a line of fluorescent is concealed. During the day, natural light is diffused through the translucent shade, and at night the blackout shade is dropped to create almost a light-box effect, adding general light to the kitchen.

OPPOSITE LEFT These thick shelves are spaced about 2½ in. (60mm) from the wall, and a continuous line of slimline fluorescent has been used to provide a backlit effect, so that the light washes up and down the white wall silhouetting the books. A recessed downlight in the ceiling provides a soft wash of light, which is just sufficient to soften the silhouette effect and light up the spines of the books.

OPPOSITE RIGHT There are four distinct lighting effects at play in this living room. The general light comes from the uplight—fluorescent during the day and a rope light at night—concealed above the timber and stone wall. Similar sources have been used behind the long, low bench to uplight the wall, providing a "horizon line." The fluorescent source is used by day and early evening, changing to the rope light, with its soft yellow candlelike glow, at night. The stone recesses are lit with low-voltage halogen using 27-deg. lamps set into the wood overhang. In the main ceiling, the trimless rectangular minigrid is used to accent objects on the low bench and light the back of the sofa, almost as a reading light.

Concealed lighting is a particularly effective solution in a minimalist architectural setting, as these spaces often benefit from being lit discreetly with no visible light sources. The clean, crisp lines of such interiors can be enhanced and accentuated by strips of concealed lighting.

Working out where to locate the light sources is key. To provide general light, one solution is a recessed cove in the ceiling, so the light is concealed by an upstand and the light reflects off the ceiling. For this to be effective, there needs to be a minimum depth of $1\frac{3}{4}$ inches (200mm) from the ceiling. When creating accent lighting to uplight a feature such as a doorway or arch, providing extra definition within the space, the key is to use an uplight in which the source is well recessed within the fixture. This means the light source is recessed by a minimum of 2 inches (50mm), and a narrow-beam lamp is used to prevent glare as you walk by.

"**When concealing a light source, remember that it may at some stage need to be maintained, so make sure that it is not too difficult to reach.**"

Task lighting

Once the background lighting has been planned and points of interest brought into focus with accent lighting, the next thing to think about is the functional lighting needed to perform certain tasks, whether this is cooking, desk work, or reading in bed.

This type of functional lighting is known as "task lighting." While background lighting establishes the general light levels in a room, and accent lighting adds points of focus and creates mood, task lighting is essential for carrying out practical functions. In utility rooms and kitchens, a bright light will be required over working areas, such as sinks, stoves, and countertops; in bathrooms, an even, flattering light is essential for applying makeup and shaving; a home office or desk space requires good general light to prevent eye strain and a dedicated desk light for close work; in living rooms and bedrooms, a reading light is usually necessary. In some instances, the background lighting may provide enough light for the task to be performed, but when it is dimmed, this will no longer be the case, and another light effect will be required.

The first thing to consider are the various tasks that need to be performed within your home. In the kitchen, it is the preparation and cooking of food, and all that entails. Depending on the layout, focus may be required on a countertop beneath wall-mounted cabinets, and the answer may be to have fluorescent, low-voltage, or LED sources fitted onto the underside of the units. The choice of light source depends on how the light can be concealed, whether the heat from the light source would have an impact on the cupboards above, and whether

OPPOSITE The lamp on the chest, with its simple white shade, brings a soft glow to the room, adding to the general light and the ambiance, but not providing sufficient light by which to read. The simple bronze light on the other side of the armchair fulfills this role, providing a soft directional light at just the right height for reading a book or newspaper. There are several designs of this type of light. Some are adjustable in height, and others have pivoting arms that can be swung around to focus the light in the correct position.

LEFT In the corner of this library, a reading light provides directional light over an armchair and side table. A light such as this can be used to introduce a pocket of light into a room that can be used to highlight the fabric on a sofa or a piece of sculpture on a side table, and can then be redirected for reading when required. It is a good additional light for a room in which there are already several lamps—where another lamp shade may be just too busy, the concealed glow from this shielded light source is perfect.

LEFT The articulated arm on this floor-standing fixture allows the angle of the light to be redirected to wherever it is required. This type of fixture provides a flexible solution in a tight space, as the light can be angled over a desk or, as here, over a chair for reading. The utilitarian design suits the mood of this loft space.

BELOW LEFT This desk light is another space-saving solution. The base of the light can be clamped securely onto the edge of a desk, and the angle of the arm adjusted to focus the light source wherever it is needed. The deep bowl-shaped metal shade helps to reduce glare.

OPPOSITE TOP The stainless-steel niche in the center of this black kitchen is the focus of the cooking area. It is lit from above using two 20W 12V downlights recessed in the soffit above, which also houses the ventilation fan. The lights create sparkle on the stovetop and surrounding surface.

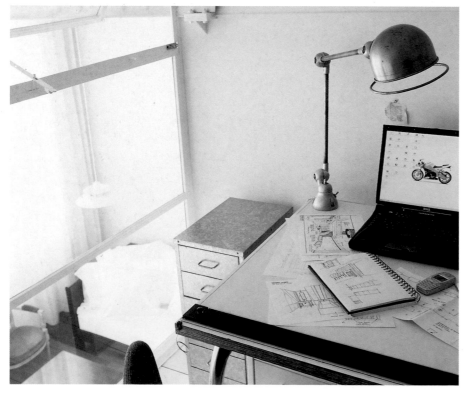

the countertop is polished or not. Avoid a continuous light source above a polished countertop, as it will result in unwanted reflections. If you need a direct light over a kitchen island, this could be provided by a decorative pendant or downlights located overhead. (See pages 54–5 and 56.) Whatever the solution, any task lights should always be controlled on a separate circuit from the other lighting effects so that they can be dimmed or switched off entirely when you wish to create a softer mood that is more conducive to dining.

Effective lighting for reading or writing is best achieved with a local, freestanding desk or table lamp that can be focused exactly where light is needed. As long as the receptacles are placed in the right location, the choice of the task light can come later and will depend largely on the style of the interior. Sometimes an overhead light is preferred, which can work well over a desk, but not over a sofa, as it is not a flattering light to sit directly under.

In a bedroom, a decorative bedside light may help to define the look of the room and add to the mood, but often this will not provide adequate light for reading. In this case, a small directional light attached to the wall or headboard may be the solution, with independent controls on each side of the bed.

In a bathroom or dressing room, a good, flattering light is necessary for shaving or applying makeup. The key is to achieve an even, shadow-free light on the face, and this is usually best obtained by lighting each side of a mirror. A light inside a closet or cabinet is also desirable so that you can easily see the contents at a glance.

LEFT 20W 12V flexilights are located on a wood backdrop behind the sink. The light source is completely shielded from direct glare, and the flexible "neck" of the fixture, similar to a shower hose, can be manipulated in any direction. Here, it is used to focus on the stainless-steel sink and countertop below. This is an ideal solution for task lighting in a kitchen where there are no cabinets under which to fit downlights and no possibility of ceiling lights.

BELOW LEFT This kitchen sink is located in a central island where any localized lighting is impossible. Instead, recessed downlights positioned directly above the island and controlled separately from the room's general downlights are an ideal solution. The lights' reflections on the stainless steel add a wonderful glow, creating a feature in the workspace.

"Task lighting should always be controlled by a separate circuit from the other light effects in the room so that it can be switched off when a soft mood setting is required."

Decorative lighting

Purely a personal and aesthetic choice, decorative lights can form part of the general or mood lighting in a room or simply add a special effect. There are many options available to suit any style of interior.

chandeliers

With the reintroduction of decoration and pattern in interior design after the pared-down minimalism of the 1990s, the chandelier has found itself back in fashion once again. There are many stunning designs available, both traditional in style and contemporary examples, with faceted crystals that give off the most sparkle, as well as smooth droplets, lenses, and tubes that appear to glow from within. In various shapes and sizes, from dramatic spirals and theatrical cascades to simple branches and tiers, they are an obvious way to bring a decorative light effect into a room and provide instant focus.

Conventionally, chandeliers were centrally located, and often they were the only source of light within a room. Now more often considered as one element in a lighting scheme made up of many different effects, chandeliers can still be effective as a central feature, over a dining table or in a high-ceiling hallway, for example. Don't let this limit your imagination—the effect can be dramatic and surprising when they are used in unexpected settings, such as in a bathroom suspended over a bathtub, or hung in the corner of a room as a feature light. Chandeliers can even be used on either side of a bed as an alternative to a bedside light, which is a particularly effective solution where space is restricted.

Bear in mind, when choosing a chandelier for a room, that an overscaled decorative fixture will always create more drama. A chandelier that is too small for the space will look apologetic and will not deliver the impact it should.

OPPOSITE The wonderful glass-bowl chandelier is made up of hundreds of glass lenses fixed together. The incandescent source within is refracted through the glass to create interesting points of light. The glamorous chandelier is the focus and general light in this setting, but there are two other effects in the background. Two metal Anglepoise® lamps provide focused task light on either side of the desk, and three directional spots are used on each of the shelving units to provide a wash of light down the front of the shelves. The objects displayed on the shelves have been moved to the front edges because they would otherwise be in shadow from the shelf above. This is the accent light in the room.

ABOVE RIGHT This pretty, feminine crystal and metal chandelier has simple candle-shaped incandescent lamps. It is important that a clear lamp is used and not a pearl one, as it is the filament point source that creates the sparkle against the crystal chandelier. As traditional incandescent lamps are being slowly phased out, the pressure is on lightbulb manufacturers to develop a point source substitute. This chandelier could be made to sparkle even more by directing two small low-voltage downlights through the crystal. This technique means the candle lamps on the chandelier itself can be dimmed, while the crystal is highlighted by the downlight. It works especially well in a dining room because it focuses light on the table below.

RIGHT This unusual chandelier is made up of hundreds of interconnecting twisted glass tubes, which can be hooked together to form almost any shape. This fixture has three inner rings from which to start the process, creating a tiered effect reminiscent of a wedding cake. The light source in the center is softly filtered through the layers.

> "Use clear incandescent bulbs in crystal chandeliers, as the crystal reflects the filament and creates more sparkle."

ABOVE A traditional branched chandelier with crystal drops hangs in front of a stark central fireplace, providing an interesting juxtaposition of styles and textures. The decorative nature of the light fixture brings an unexpected touch of glamour to the otherwise pared-down contemporary surroundings. The play of light from a chandelier is often the only decorative element needed.

ABOVE RIGHT This large spiral crystal chandelier has an internal light source that is multilayered, so there is light at every level. This is important in creating a glow through the entire fixture. This dramatic chandelier needs to be hung from a high ceiling because of its size and would work well in a double-height space, creating a stunning focal point and visual statement. Chandeliers such as this also work well suspended low in the corner of a room for a dramatic effect.

OPPOSITE TOP This circular chandelier, made up of smooth crystal droplets, is a contemporary take on a traditional chandelier. The light tends to glow rather than sparkle because there are no cut edges on the crystal pieces. For a high-impact sparkle, select a chandelier with lots of faceted drops, such as the traditional Baccarat ones and those from Swarovski crystal. If a more low-key effect is required, an example such as this is beautiful and subtle. It has a line of incandescent bulbs within it that sparkle through the glass. Being circular, it offers the opportunity to add a downlight in the center on a second circuit, which would add a wonderful accent effect on any object or table positioned below it.

OPPOSITE BOTTOM This long, curved design, with uncut bulbous pear-shaped drops, is an interesting modern take on a traditional chandelier. It would work especially well suspended low over a rectangular dining table, providing a soft, atmospheric light and a flattering sparkling effect.

"For maximum sparkle, choose a chandelier with multifaceted crystal drops, which will reflect and refract the light the most, creating decorative effects and throwing wonderful patterns of color and shadow onto the walls, floor, and ceiling."

pendant lights

In the past, a central pendant was often the only source of lighting within a room, but it is now widely acknowledged that the quality of light from a single source is insufficient and results in an all-over general light that is flat and uninteresting. In addition, light from a single central source can also be glaring, leaving everything it does not reach in darkness. This means that too much work is done by one light source alone.

Modern pendants are rarely the only light source in a room and come in any number of guises in metal, wood, plastic, paper, or fabric. Much like a chandelier, a statement pendant not only contributes to the buildup of lighting effects within a room, but also plays an important part in creating the mood of the interior—it is part of the decoration and reinforces the look of the room. Often, while the same discreet lighting effects can be applied to any style of interior, it is the choice of decorative light that sets the mood and tone. For example, by whatever means the general light is produced in a room, the addition of a modern pendant will create a completely different feel to that of the same interior with a traditional crystal chandelier. A pendant light creates a statement, so it often gives the impression that it is doing all the work—yet it is the architectural or concealed solutions that are producing the general light.

While a pendant light can literally be the decorative centerpiece in a room, these days it is not limited to being used in this way. It can be dramatically suspended in a corner or dropped low over a table or kitchen island to provide task lighting. Pendants can also replace conventional bedside lamps or wall

LEFT This unusual pendant suspended centrally over a dining table is like a cylindrical sculpture. The light source is concealed in a dish in the base of the fixture, providing a wonderful uplight effect that catches the metalwork and reflects off the ceiling.

RIGHT Three simple pendants made of split-curved wood hang in a line above a kitchen island. The light source is concealed in the "neck" of the fixture and sends light down to provide a soft glow on the surface below. The split wood, lit on the sides only, creates a wonderful pattern of light and dark.

LEFT Lighting a mirror evenly on both sides provides the most flattering light for the face. This is achieved here through a combination of the elegant pendant fixtures, which provide a refreshing change to ubiquitous wall lights, and a fluorescent source inserted behind the mirror, which provides a soft backlight that also reflects off the two side walls.

OPPOSITE LEFT This linen shade diffuses the light to a warm glow. Any glare is prevented by the covered base, but the small aperture in the center means that some direct light is still able to go downward.

OPPOSITE RIGHT The dramatic pendant hanging over a stairwell almost resembles a tiered wedding cake. The shade gives a warm effect—like light diffused through parchment—but it is actually made of lots of fine pieces of porcelain, which achieves the wonderful soft light. Each piece is handmade, giving the light a unique feel.

lights, with the light source suspended low down, at the level of a table lamp, thereby freeing up space on the bedside table. (See page 123.)

The key with any decorative lighting is to know what the light source is at the planning stage. If it is a bare light source, it will need to be dimmable so it does not create glare and distract from the fixture itself (remember, the eye is always drawn to the brightest point). A light source with a soft shade, however, will need to be dimmed less. Many interesting pendants have been created by the play of light diffusing through material. If the shade is dark, light is directed almost entirely up and down, but if the shade is diffuse, like a parchment shade, it may show the pattern of the fabric or provide a soft outward light. If more than one type of decorative light is used in the same space, particularly if one has a bare light source and the other does not, then they should be wired on separate circuits and controlled separately. The light produced by a glass chandelier or lantern that will need to be dimmed will be very different compared with a shaded pendant that gives off a glow of light similar to a table lamp.

RIGHT An elegant pair of sconces frames an entrance, emitting a soft glow through the parchment shades that give the light a yellow quality. The long, shardlike bronze bases add strength to the relatively small shades, making them ideal statement lights for a narrow location. The wall lights create a soft indirect glow that lights the painting by Susan Jayne Hocking on the adjacent wall.

OPPOSITE LEFT This is one of a pair of sconces that frame a bathroom mirror, primarily casting light downward. This creates a moody atmosphere, but makes them impractical task lights, as no sideways light is thrown at the face.

OPPOSITE TOP RIGHT This pretty double wall sconce is a French piece from the twentieth century, useful for creating a small pocket of light within a scheme.

OPPOSITE BOTTOM RIGHT These sconces are traditionally used in libraries, as they can easily be adjusted for reading. Here, they are used to frame an arched alcove window, making the window seat seem more inviting and creating a quiet corner in which to read.

sconces

Traditional sconces are a form of candelabra with exposed lamps, the effect of which can be softened by the addition of shades.

Modern interpretations offer an endless choice of designs. Sconces can be used to frame an entrance, as bedside lights where space is limited and there is no room for a table lamp, or mounted on a bookcase to provide soft infill light to the surrounding shelves without lighting them directly. They are also another means by which to create pockets of light as part of the layering of effects in an overall scheme. (See page 94.) Decorative wall lights can be substitutes for freestanding lamps and should be mounted at eye level—5½–5¾ feet (1.65–1.75m) above the floor, although this can vary according to the ceiling height. Architectural up-and-downlights should be fixed at the same height, while a pure uplight wall fixture needs to be above eye level, usually 6½–7 feet (1.95–2.1m) above the floor.

"Wall lights are usually decorative, so they make an important visual statement within the interior and need to be selected accordingly."

RIGHT This unusual French sconce has been made from rods of glass that diffuse the light in a wonderful way and reduce the glare from the lamp.

FAR RIGHT The hand-blown frosted-glass shade, on a patinated bronze bracket, gives a soft glow in all directions, making it ideal for introducing a soft layer of light at mid level.

OPPOSITE LEFT A traditional candle sconce uses a small clear candle bulb. Just as with lanterns and chandeliers, it is important that the bulb is clear, so that when it is dimmed it takes on a candlelike appearance. A frosted-glass bulb would not give the same sense of sparkle.

OPPOSITE RIGHT This slim tube-shaped up-and-downlight is an architectural lighting device that has two low-voltage light sources and sends a defined shaft of light both up and down. The shape of this arc of light will depend on whether a wide- or narrow-beam lamp is used. The fixture's dramatic effect makes it suitable to use outside to frame an entrance, while several can be used in a row within a hallway with striking results.

Wall light tips

Beware of using wall-mounted uplights on stairs. While they look fine as you walk up the stairs, you are likely to be dazzled by the glare from the light source when on the descent.

A sconce with an up-and-downlight fixture can be used on staircases, as the uplight tends to be of a narrow distribution and can be shielded to avoid glare.

A task-orientated sconce will often have a metal shade that focuses the light downward, making it suitable for use over a desk or as a bedside reading light. Such lights may also be mounted on a wall in a kitchen to light the countertop below.

An uplight providing background light designed to reflect off of the ceiling should be positioned at approximately 6½ ft (2m) above the fixed floor level so that it is above eye level, as the light source is usually bright.

freestanding lamps

These are the plug-in version of sconces and are often a feature of living rooms, in particular, where they are used to create localized pools of light. In most living rooms, it is the freestanding lamp that provides the background general light, usually in the form of a table lamp positioned on either side of the sofa or on a side table.

There has been a huge resurgence of interest in decorative light sources, and consequently there is a wide range of lamp bases available in anything from glass, ceramic, metal, wood, leather, or indeed almost any material. One of the greatest developments has been in freestanding floor lamps, which until recently were considered somewhat unfashionable and could be found only in traditional interiors. Many new and exciting designs have become available—some take inspiration from period designs, such as art deco, while others are the creations of contemporary artists who make wonderful sculptural bases. Many retro designs, such as the imposing Flos Arco lamp that swoops over in an elegant wide curve, are having a renaissance in modern interiors. The result is that floor lamps can now be considered stunning additions to any contemporary home and used to make a style statement in their own right. For the lighting designer, this means that there are even more tools to play with in the lighting box.

BELOW LEFT The two lamps on the console table create balance and focus in this space. The dark shades mean the light can only go up and down, which is effective for lighting the glass lamp bases and uplighting the picture on the wall behind.

BELOW This unusual lamp is almost a piece of sculpture. The hand-blown Murano frosted-glass shade glows, giving out a soft light in all directions. With this type of lamp, the key is to use a low-wattage light source and even to dim the fixture to soften the effect.

OPPOSITE Light catches this silver-glazed lamp base and reflects off of the polished surface. The pale card shade allows light to diffuse through it, providing a soft, flattering side light for the seating area next to it.

"With freestanding lamps, the choice of shade is critical in determining the resulting light effect. A fabric or translucent shade diffuses light softly through its sides, while a solid, dark shade sends shafts of light up and down."

OPPOSITE LEFT Glass lamp bases have become increasingly popular. These can be ribbed, colored, or handblown, and become pieces of art in their own right. The dark card shade means that light is focused downward over the base, to accentuate the detail in the glass.

OPPOSITE BELOW A floor lamp is an ideal solution for creating a soft light in a bedroom, where relaxation is the main aim. This simple example has a card shade, which gives a soft side light, and directs light down over the chaise longue and up the drapes, also lighting the photograph by Henri Cartier-Bresson. The oak lamp base has beautiful bronze detailing which glimmers in the light.

BELOW This 1940s French floor lamp has a unique bronze base that is as imposing as a piece of sculpture. The pale cream drum-shaped shade sends light in all directions, highlighting the shape of the striking base.

BELOW RIGHT Here, two 1940s iron floor lamps frame a sofa, allowing the same quality of light as two table lamps, but without the clutter of side tables. The dark glazed linen shades do not diffuse light sideways in the way that pale cream shades would but tend to distribute it up and down, giving a soft light that emphasizes the weave and texture of the linen.

RIGHT This adjustable floor-standing task light positioned over the corner of a sofa is a mid-century leather-wrapped design by Jacques Adnet. Its solid shade casts a direct beam of light downward, making this floor lamp ideal as a task light.

Top tips

The effect produced by a freestanding light is largely governed by the material of the shade. A freestanding task light, for example, will usually have a solid shade to ensure that the light is directed exactly where it is needed. For a decorative infill-light source positioned on either side of a sofa to provide general lighting in a living room, a pale diffuse shade will give a soft side light that is flattering to skin tones.

Think carefully about the shape of the shade, too, as this will make a design statement in the room. A cylindrical or square shade will create a more contemporary effect than an old-fashioned Empire shape. Changing the shade is an easy way to give an old lamp base a new look.

Position floor lamps carefully so that there is no glare, and the light source itself can't be seen from the seating area. Some designs can be fitted with a diffuser to soften the direct glare from the lamp.

It can be effective to use lamps symmetrically, such as in pairs on a console table or on either side of a sofa, but sometimes it can be more interesting to create different layers of lighting by having a floor lamp in a corner and low-level table lamps by the seating area.

It is important that the style of lamp reflects the interior design, as it will be the visual focus of light within the room and may be the only visible source, even though there will be lots of other light effects at work.

ABOVE LEFT This freestanding floor light is ideal as a task light over a desk, but its head can also be tilted toward the wall to create a wall-wash effect or upward to create an uplight effect.

ABOVE The design of this classic studio lamp, Fortuny, is based on the traditional photographer's light. It is ideal for creating a sculptural feature in the corner of a spacious room. The light source is concealed by the central black disk, which reflects it back onto the large white reflector. In turn, this reflects the light into the room in a soft, diffuse way. The reflector can be tilted, depending on where you want the light to be focused.

OPPOSITE LEFT This adjustable floor lamp is perfect for use beside a sofa or chair, especially when there is no room for a side table. The diffusing cream shade gives a flattering side light, and the light can also be brightened for reading. It is important to have a frosted-acrylic disk below the lamp to prevent direct glare.

As is the case with pendants and wall lights, the choice of shade for a freestanding lamp is critical in determining the effect and quality of the light it provides, which will vary significantly depending on the material, color, and shape of the shade. A cream or parchment shade will produce a soft, warm glow of light, whereas a blue or green shade will result in a much cooler light that is often less sympathetic to an interior and less flattering to skin tone. Lining a shade with gold or silver will have similar effects on the light—it will appear warmer reflected off the gold shade and cooler reflected off the silver. A shade made from dense or solid material that is not translucent will not diffuse the light, but will instead direct it up and down, producing a harsher, less-flattering effect.

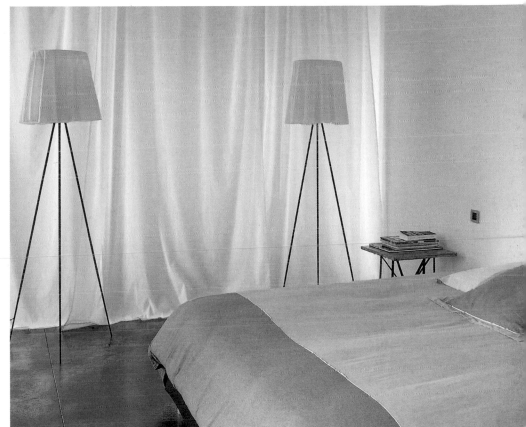

ABOVE RIGHT The simple, unobtrusive tripod lamps work well in this minimalist all-white interior. The unusual folds on the diffuse white shades work well against the soft folds of the curtain.

RIGHT This fluorescent tube, casually positioned against the wall, is like a piece of light sculpture, reminiscent of the work of light artist Dan Flavin. Here, the fluorescent is capped at both ends and has a green sleeve around the tube, which gives the green hue. Other colors could be used to create different effects.

Layering

A good, flexible lighting scheme is made up of several types of lights that produce a variety of effects. These can be combined in different ways and at various levels of intensity, according to changing needs and natural light throughout the day.

"Layering" may seem an unusual term to use in relation to lighting, but in the same way as an interior designer builds up layers of color, texture, and finishes to achieve the final scheme, a lighting designer plays with a combination of different lighting effects, selecting each one to fulfill a practical need or to create a specific visual impact and different plays of light and shadow.

Good layering is built of many different light effects, each introduced at different levels or positions. For example, if there is a pendant in the room at one level, try to introduce an uplight or a low-level floor washer and a mid-level light, which could be a wall light, a lit bookshelf, or a lit picture. Make sure that each of these types of light can be controlled independently so that different moods can easily be achieved by altering their intensities.

Understanding how to layer light and recognizing which effects work well together are key to good lighting. A successful and flexible scheme depends on a balanced combination of all the individual effects discussed in the previous pages. It doesn't matter whether the interior is traditional or contemporary, the idea of layering effects and creating pockets of light within the room is crucial for the best result, and the same rules apply in whatever style they are interpreted and in whichever room.

How to layer light

Layers of light are built by considering the different types of background lighting, task lighting, and feature lighting. Decide on the effects you would like to employ to produce these—wall washing, floor washing, downlighting, or uplighting, for instance—and use them in different proportions and intensities depending on the balance required in the room. Bear in mind that in one situation the light effect may be a background light, but used with a different source it can provide a more direct light and become an accent light. For example:

Light should be introduced from different directions. If the general lighting is uplighting, providing a soft diffuse effect reflecting light off of the ceiling, try to use a specific downlight for the accent light, whether this is focusing on a table or piece of art. Then use a localized lamp to add a soft infill light at mid level.

Another contrasting solution would be to use recessed downlights for a wall-washing effect to create reflected light off the walls as background light; then to add recessed narrow-beam uplights to pick out some of the features and provide accent lighting. In this instance, with the majority of the lighting focused around the walls, a chandelier or narrow-beam downlight could be used to create a central focus.

If the background lighting in a room is provided by freestanding decorative lamps, then the feature lighting may be a combination of narrow-beam uplights used to define architectural features and low-voltage downlights to highlight pictures or create a focus in the center of the room.

The hallway is the central focus of this open-plan penthouse apartment, linking both ends of the space together. The lighting is built up of various elements, each contributing to the overall impact. First there is the infill general light from the low-glare downlights in the ceiling, one of which is directed onto the orchid on the table. Next is the lighting on either side, made up of the individual lighting on each shelf. This creates a soft side light similar to a wall light. Additional focus is provided by the dramatic architraves surrounding the doorway to the master bedroom. (See page 37.) In the niches between the shelving, discreet low-glare uplights are used to emphasize the curved shape. These niches will eventually house sculptures, which will be thrown into dramatic silhouette. At the far end is a magnificent fireplace with two recessed uplights that emphasize its sides and catch on and reflect off the mantelpiece. In the center of the hallway is a skylight that brings natural light into the middle of the apartment. In order to prevent this from appearing as a dark hole at night, small 20W 12V starlights (bare capsule lamps in a chrome housing) have been installed on the vertical edge to create a glow. When the glass is black, these are reflected as tiny, starlike point sources.

"The most creative and flexible lighting schemes are usually made up of many different light effects, or layers, of lights. These need to be controlled independently from one another, so that they can be used together, in various combinations, and at different intensities."

OPPOSITE TOP This dressing area has two key lighting effects at work. The first is the use of 20W 12V starlight fixtures mounted on a chrome base and fixed onto the mirror. These provide a good, even light for the face, as well as the artwork, *Feathers* by Linda Bird. When off, they almost disappear into the mirror. Below the countertop, xenon strip lighting gives a soft wash over the stool and floor, lighting an area that would otherwise be in darkness. A similar effect can be achieved with an LED lighting strip.

OPPOSITE BOTTOM This entrance hall has three key lighting effects and, in essence, two layers. The first effect is the lit focal points that immediately draw the eye—the picture on the end wall, *A Fitting at de Blausse's* by K Baumgartner, the flowers on the sideboard, and the pictures on either side of it. The second effect is provided by the lamps, which, because of their dark, solid shades, cast light up and down. The final infill effect comes from some central downlights that have been dimmed to a low level.

RIGHT This corner of a living room illustrates three layers of light. The first is the table lamp, providing a soft infill glow and visual focus. The second is the scallop from the downlight over the blind, repeated across the window. Finally, the shelves themselves are backlit, which creates the strong horizontal bands of light on the wall behind. Each individual effect helps to build up the different layers within the scheme. One effect alone would light the room, but would not introduce the level of interest or detail that is achieved by layering several effects.

SPOTLIGHT ON a dining area within an imposing high-ceilinged reception room, where a combination of light effects is at work at different levels. In any room, lighting should be used to form pools and pockets of light that help to create atmosphere, and this is particularly crucial in large, open spaces, where lighting plays an important role in defining zones and engendering a feeling of coziness and warmth.

Pendant light

The visual focus is provided by the hanging lantern, which is the obvious statement light and makes a traditional stylistic reference point. As the scheme is made up of several different lighting effects, the lantern does not have to do all the work and can be dimmed to a decorative glow. It uses incandescent sources so that, when it is dimmed, it has a warm glow like candlelight. Dimming a decorative source makes it a far softer element within the interior. If it is too bright, the light source itself becomes the focus, rather than the surrounding pool of light that it creates.

Downlight

The silk drapes are lit with a discreet low-voltage directional downlight with a wide-beam 40-deg. 35W 12V lamp. This effect softly outlines the perimeter of the room, highlighting the texture of the material, and at the same time, adding a soft infill general light to the edges of the room. This light source can be controlled individually, and making it bright will increase the feeling of space within the room, as the eye is drawn to the outer perspective. Dimming the source very low will make the room appear smaller, as the focus remains in the center while the perimeter is almost in darkness.

Spotlights

In any room, it is effective to have a central focus that catches the eye. The wooden dining table is in the center of this room, and three narrow pools of light highlight its surface. The orchid at one end of the table catches and reflects the narrow beam of light from above. Although bright, the 8-deg. narrow-beam light sources are shielded from direct view, so the brightest point becomes the orchid, which draws the eye toward it.

Uplight

The column capital is uplit by narrow-beam fiber-optic lights located at the column base. Fiber optics were selected because there was a depth of only about 2½ in. (60mm) to set the light into, while the light box could be housed in the base of the bookshelf. The effect of the pool of light is to emphasize the height of the column and provide a degree of soft reflected light off of the ceiling. These uplights contrast with the downlight effect on the bookcase and curtains.

Table lamp

The lamp on the side table, like the lantern, is a clearly recognizable lighting reference point. It is not lit to full brightness, so its effect is not glaring. The pool of light on the drapes behind appears to come from the lamp, rather than the discreet downlights that are actually doing the work. This is another level of infill light at mid level, adding to the overall harmony of the scheme in which each effect is controlled individually to balance the various layers of light.

ABOVE The overall view of this room is created through many individual lighting elements, or layers, of light. They all work together and are controlled individually to achieve the perfect balance. Each on their own would not provide sufficient light, but together they create an interesting and beautiful room. At first glance, the main light sources appear to be the lantern and table lamp, but actually there are many other different effects at work, as described, opposite.

LIGHTING IN PRACTICE: ROOM BY ROOM

Every space within a home has different lighting needs and requirements. Some are practical and some are decorative, but they all need to be addressed in order to achieve the best results possible. The way each room is treated will depend on a number of factors—its type and size, whether it is part of an open plan or if the ceiling is vaulted, double-height, how much natural light it receives, the main functions that are carried out there, and the time of day it is mainly used. In addition, the style of interior plays a significant role.

Living rooms

The living room is probably the most sociable room in the home. It's where the family gathers and where friends are entertained, but it's also a room for relaxing, whether watching television, listening to music, or reading. Above all, the lighting needs to be flexible, with each effect controlled separately to change the mood.

Of all the rooms in the home, the living room is usually the one where the background light is provided by table or floor lamps, and occasionally by chandeliers and pendants. In order for freestanding lamps to provide the appropriate level of lighting, it is essential to position them in the correct place—and it is crucial to ensure that you have sufficient power outlets from the outset. For this reason, it is sensible to plan the layout of furniture first. For example, in a large room you will need receptacles located in the floor, which can be hidden underneath the sofas. This may seem obvious, but it is all too often forgotten. Lamps that are placed around the perimeter of the room can leave a dark hole in the center. The choice of shade has an impact on the quality of light emitted. (See pages 83 and 92.) A solid shade will provide a sharp up-and-downlight with no light at the sides, whereas a diffuse parchment or fabric shade will provide a soft side light which is more flattering.

Chandeliers and pendants can also be used to provide the infill light in a living area, often making a dramatic style statement in their own right. (See pages 77–83.) They are particularly effective in rooms with very high ceilings, as they have the effect of visually reducing the scale and lowering the ceiling. For this reason, in rooms that have lower ceilings, pendants and chandeliers are usually best used away from the center of the room. Instead, think about suspending them low over a table or even in a corner of a room, in the place of a floor lamp. Using a pendant in an unusual and unexpected manner can be a fun way to introduce a new layer of lighting.

RIGHT This large living room appears to be classically lit by table lamps, which are behind both sofas and give a soft general light. There are, however, other effects at play. Small low-level uplights emphasize each corner of the room and the crown molding. Another pocket of light is created by the soft uplight behind the pots on the Chinese cabinet. (See page 64.) In the foreground, the key focus is the detail on the fireplace. This is lit with two uplights on either side, a technique that ensures the fireplace remains a focal point in the room even when the fire itself is not lit. (See page 18.)

In very minimalist interiors, the clutter of decorative light fixtures may seem to be too much. But rather than just opting for downlights—sitting directly under a downlight is always unpleasant—try instead to use some of the ideas suggested in Concealed Lighting. (See page 66.) For example, a soft wash of light on a wall from a concealed linear source in a recess or an indirect light from recessed uplights.

The next thing to consider is task lighting, which, in a living room, is needed for reading. The best solution is a local adjustable task light, which is preferable to an overhead downlight, as it can be angled as required.

Skillfully used, downlights can provide magical effects in living rooms, but are best employed here for accent lighting. Lighting a favorite picture with an adjustable light fitted with the correct beam angle can produce wonderful focus. There are various options of lamps and lenses from 10–60 degrees, so the perfect result is not hard to achieve. As ever, be careful to select downlights that have the light source well recessed to prevent direct glare. In period interiors, a picture light may be the best solution for bringing focus to a piece of art.

Accent lighting can also include highlighting features, such as a fireplace, which can be achieved by means of recessed or freestanding uplights. This helps to create interest whenever the fire is not lit, especially during the summer months. Another effect that really creates impact is to introduce light into the center of a room, by focusing a downlight onto a coffee table, for instance. This instantly makes the space feel welcoming and draws you into the room.

OPPOSITE AND ABOVE This inspired conversion of a Victorian home retains the proportions of the two front rooms, but has a double-height space at the back, created by removing the floor of the room above. An ingenious glass-and-metal staircase replaces the original enclosed stairs, allowing light to filter through to the bottom of the house. At night, the lighting effects unify the various zones and make the space come alive. The staircase is uplit from below, catching the frosted-glass treads. Each landing is lit by a recessed floor washer, which means that the entrance of the house is lit by the glowing glass landings above. A small low-voltage black track is concealed by the steel supporting the glass bridge. This produces a soft wall wash that lights the photographs, *The Waves* by Daška Hatton, and reflects light into the room. In the kitchen/dining area, the general light is from the uplights above the cabinets. To contrast with this effect, skillfully placed downlights highlight the kitchen island and the center of the dining table. In the room above, the soft indirect light washing across the ceiling comes from the backlit shelves, while small recessed downlights highlight the fronts of the bookcase. (See also pages 15 and 71.)

Top tips for living rooms

Before any decisions on lighting are made, plan how the seating will be arranged and decide what will be the focal points of the room.

A painting, *objet d' art*, or piece of furniture, such as a central coffee table, can be accentuated subtly and with stunning effect by a recessed directional downlight. Different lenses can be used in front of the bulb to give a variety of effects. If it is impossible to use recessed lights, then a plug-in solution such as a surface-mounted spot could be the answer.

In a large living room, add floor receptacles so that you can bring light into the center of the room. These should be located where they will be hidden under furniture. Always provide ample receptacles in the corners of the room, too, as additional lighting is often required. Do not add too many lamps, however, or the room will look cluttered.

A simple uplight hidden in a corner behind a piece of furniture can add an extra dimension, making the space seem bigger and highlighting any molding on the ceiling.

Consider lighting a bookcase or display shelving. This can be done in a number of ways—for example, lighting through glass shelves; lighting shelves from the front; backlighting shelves to throw the objects into silhouette; or highlighting specific items displayed.

Don't forget task lighting if you like to read in the living room. A dedicated plug-in reading light, ideally one with an articulated head that can be angled where you need it, is best.

Before you start

When designing the lighting for a living room, it is essential to think about how the room is going to be used. Write a checklist of all the elements that need to be considered.

1 What will the general lighting be?

2 What will the focused lighting be? On what elements in the room will the accent lighting be focusing? This could be anything from pictures, *objets d' art*, and architectural details, to furniture.

3 How do you intend to add extra layers of lighting to provide softness and create a welcoming mood? In a living room, this is often best achieved with freestanding lamps, while statement pendant lights or chandeliers are also good additions. Other possible options are to introduce indirect light from undershelf lighting or recessed linear uplights, providing a soft wall-wash effect.

4 The final element to consider is how the various lighting effects are to be controlled. Each effect needs to have its own individual control, which can be operated either by a standard rotary control or by a more sophisticated preset scene control. In the case of the latter, each circuit is individually balanced to different levels for each scene (usually four), so that the perfect scene can be selected at the touch of a button. (See pages 40–41 and 171.)

ABOVE LEFT The slot fireplace is the focus of this contemporary living room. The strong shafts of downlight on each stone panel create a visual effect and also reflect light into the room. The infill background light is from a soft uplight above the wooden surround. To add to the layers of light, a recessed double downlight creates a pool of light over the coffee table, drawing together the seating area and making it feel more welcoming.

LEFT A light source is concealed behind the low bench to create a soft uplight with a horizon effect, which also throws the objects placed on the bench into silhouette. The picture above, *Grey Forest* by Anna Pales, is lit with a pair of 50W 12V rectangular fittings that focus the light in the center, highlighting the horizon within the picture. To the left, table lamps provide infill light, while a linear LED source with elongating lenses directs shafts of light down the drapes, which are set in a recess. The advantage of the LED strip is that it emits little heat, so it can be located close to the drape fabric.

> "Decide on the layout of furniture, artworks, and any other key focal points within the living room before you plan the lighting. This way, you will ensure that you use the best light effects for each area in the room, and install sufficient power outlets wherever they are needed."

ABOVE RIGHT This welcoming corner of a living room appears to be simply lit with ambient light from a table lamp. In fact, there are three other sources of light. Discreet low-glare recessed downlights in the ceiling (out of view) focus on the artwork by Bryan Wynter above the chair with a 27-deg. medium-beam lamp, and on the circular coffee table with a 10-deg. lamp with a honeycomb louver to further reduce any glare from the light source. There are two simple plug-in solutions as well: a small 20W 12V tabletop spot at the base of the bronze sculpture to highlight the corner and project shadows onto the archway, and a task reading light beside the armchair, ideal not only for additional light to read by, but also to highlight the sculpture by Kim James on the side table. (See pages 17 and 38.)

RIGHT A table lamp gives this wonderful beamed living room a welcoming feel. A beautiful chandelier suspended over the desk provides additional general light, and the bookcases are washed with light from the customized rails mounted above, with three adjustable 20W 12V 40-deg. spotlights on each rail. A bronze 35W 12V spotlight with a 10-deg. narrow-beam lamp is focused on the white stone bowl on the glass coffee table, helping to pull the seating area together. Each effect is at a different level, to build up the scene and provide different focuses.

SPOTLIGHT ON a double-height living area with floor-to-ceiling windows in a penthouse apartment. The space needs to be lit in such as way as to enhance the stunning view of the river by night, making the most of the dramatic lighting on the bridge.

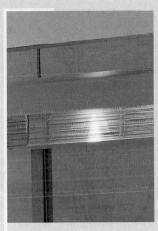

Concealed lighting

A specially designed band across the window bars contains automatic blinds that cut out the sun's glare. At night, when these are closed, they create an enclosed area in which lighting is concealed. The boxing was enlarged to hold narrow up-and-downlights that create a striking pattern on the blinds. (See below right.)

Accent lighting

The small recessed downlight in the ceiling of the mezzanine level was designed to provide a focus of light on the coffee table, effectively drawing the seating area together. Here, the 10-deg., narrow-beam lamp highlights a display of roses.

Outside lighting

The trick with windows is to light something beyond—otherwise it will appear totally black at night and reflect everything in the room. Here, the job has been done by the lighting on the bridge over the river. Who needs artwork with a nightscape such as this?

Task lighting

The classic Arco floor lamp, designed in the 1960s by Achille Castiglioni, hovers over the sofa, providing a pool of light that is bright enough to read by. When not required as a task light, its head, neatly balanced on the marble base, can be pushed away to avoid focusing light directly over the seating area.

LEFT, BELOW AND RIGHT Two large table lamps provide a visual screen between the sitting and dining areas in this open-plan space, as does the column supporting the mezzanine gallery, dramatically lit by a downlight on each side. The double-height volume of the room is accentuated by the up-and-downlighting on the blinds (see above), and complemented by the large-scale Arco lamp, which creates impact in the same way as a piece of sculpture.

Kitchens

Far more than a functional space for preparing food and cooking, the kitchen is regarded as the heart of the home and the center of family life these days. Often an inclusive open-plan space, a kitchen may be required to double as a place for eating, relaxing, and doing homework or other chores.

The kitchen has to work hard as a room to function efficiently throughout the day and accommodate all of the activities that are carried out there. As such, it is a great room in which to fully explore all the tools of lighting.

Background light is key—as the kitchen is a working area, a good level of general light is essential. In contemporary kitchens, this is often successfully provided by recessed downlights. Avoid falling into the common trap of arranging downlights in a regular grid configuration, and make sure you don't locate them only over the walkway, leaving the countertops in darkness. Look at the elevations, and relate the lighting to these. The best approach is to align the downlights with the cabinet doors, and direct the light toward their surface to achieve a soft, reflected light. If the kitchen has a central island, downlights can be used here as well, perhaps even a combination of downlights and a decorative pendant for added impact.

Another effect that works extremely well, particularly in a dark basement area or in a room with very high ceilings, is to use the tops of the cabinets for uplights that provide indirect illumination reflected off of the ceiling. It is possible to use two light sources for the uplights—energy-efficient fluorescents, for a crisp uplight effect for use during the day, and rope light, which creates a soft yellow glow for the evening. This effect is not for general light but just for mood. Uplighting can also emphasize any architectural detailing and helps to reduce the number of downlights required in the ceiling, which are often overused as a solution.

RIGHT This dramatic black-lacquered kitchen has an unusual zebrano backsplash. Its elegance makes it the perfect backdrop in an open-plan apartment. Two key lighting effects are in evidence here: one is the use of 10W 12V capsule lamps recessed under the black-lacquered units to provide a soft perimeter glow; a warm LED source could also have been used here. The second effect is the grid of low-voltage downlights focused on the island. The idea is to keep downlights to a minimum. This was possible as the white solid surfacing reflects the light back up to the ceiling, almost as an uplight would, to create more infill general light. If the countertop had been dark, this reflection would not have been possible, and more downlights would have been required. The reflective nature of a surface is an important consideration in any scheme.

LEFT This striking glass backsplash has been back-painted and lit to create a purely visual effect, rather than providing a working light. The light sources are fiber optics located at the back of the countertop, which light into the edge of the glass. They are mounted about 3 in. (75mm) below the countertop to direct light into the edge of the glass, so that the individual flares from each fiber are not visible and the light appears as a continuous line. The light box is located under the unit, where it is easily accessible. The top of the glass has a metal cap, which reflects the light below so that it appears continuous at the top edge, too.

Top tips for kitchens

Task lighting is essential in any kitchen. Use low-voltage downlights set into the underside of the cabinets to light the countertop below.

If there is a central island, use downlights above it to provide task lighting. If you are unable to recess them, create a drop effect by hanging a wire rack over the island to hang pots, and incorporate mini spotlights within this. Always control the lights over the central island on a separate circuit from the other lighting in the kitchen.

In a small or galley kitchen, downlights give a warm glow and can be used to great effect to bounce light off built-in cabinets, accentuating their color, and giving a feeling of space. If the units have attractive doors, direct the light at them so their surface is highlighted.

In a kitchen with high ceilings, the tops of cabinets can be used for uplights to provide general light. This will also reduce the number of downlights that are required.

For mood lighting, consider having lights set into the toe kick of a central island to wash light across the surface of the floor.

If the kitchen units are freestanding and so do not have a toe kick, clickstrip or LED strips can be used underneath to make them appear to float.

Bear in mind that any exposed light fixtures will collect the grime that cooking creates. If possible, choose either recessed or semirecessed fixtures.

The next thing to consider is the localized task lighting. In a galley kitchen, this is probably best provided by undercabinet lights. A variety of warmer compact fluorescent lights can work in this situation. So can low-voltage halogen lights that can be dimmed for a wonderful nighttime effect, but have the disadvantage of creating heat, which may adversely affect food stored in the cabinet above. This undercabinet effect can be brought into play when the general light has been lowered.

A central island is usually best served with a direct downlight, which can either be in the ceiling itself or built into a suspended hanging rack. Light may also be provided by decorative overhead pendant lights, which also serve to create a statement within the interior. (See pages 56 and 115.) In traditional kitchens, an overhead pendant will provide an immediate visual reference for the sort of fixture that in the past was expected to be the main source of light. These days it can be backed up with low-glare downlights.

This galley kitchen is at the center of an apartment and has no windows, so the frosted-glass backsplash is lit to mimic one. The backsplash is set 4 inches (100mm) off the rear wall, which is painted white, and overlapping fluorescents are concealed at the top and bottom to provide a continuous, even light source. Ideal as a working light during the day, at night it can appear a little harsh, and the small halogen downlights over the countertop provide a softer effect and the backlight can be switched off.

Other ideas for kitchens

For a softer, less industrial feel than downlights, use wall lights or Anglepoise® on either side of a window above a sink to provide task lighting.

Recess spotlights within the window casing above a sink or conceal them on top of cabinets, and direct the beams to crosslight the sink.

If you have a kitchen with a beamed ceiling, use the beams to conceal small low-voltage spotlights, either recessed between the beams or surface-mounted.

Introduce a shelf at high level, which can provide extra storage and hide fixtures for working light and uplights for infill general illumination.

Light any recess or shelving to add interest, particularly if the shelves are made of glass. Use surface spotlights if it is impractical to recess lights.

OPPOSITE This contemporary kitchen relies on concealed fluorescent uplighting for the general light, while two rectangular downlights over the kitchen island create pools of focused task light. Below the countertop, a warm white LED source is used to give a soft glow. This helps to "float" the chunky stone countertop, and creates a wonderful evening effect. It would not be used during the day when natural light floods into the kitchen through the window above the sink on the right (just out of view).

RIGHT This stunning kitchen fits well into the rustic setting. The immediately obvious lighting is the line of three pendant lights suspended over the island. The task light for the countertop actually comes from the two spotlights mounted on the beam above, between the pendants, and provide a more direct working light. At low level, lights have been set into the toe kick to emphasize the texture of the old floor tiles.

The next stage is to add accent lighting. This could be lighting within glass cabinets or shelving, or even lights built into a toe kick or floating kitchen cabinets. These effects should always be controlled separately and usually come into play only as part of evening mood settings.

In eat-in and open-plan kitchens, it is important to introduce a softer lighting effect, either with lamps or wall lights. Usually a focus will be created over a dining table, again controlled separately so that it can be brought up independently from any other lighting effects. The key is to focus light in the center of the table and to control it, if necessary, with glare shading so that it does not fall uncomfortably over the head of any of the diners.

"As a working area, a kitchen needs a good level of general lighting, as well as sufficient well-positioned task lighting over the sink, stove, and countertops. To create impact, accent lighting and mood effects should be brought into play only at night when the task lighting is off and the general lighting dimmed."

SPOTLIGHT ON a contemporary kitchen. A hard-working area that doubles as a family dining space needs a lighting scheme that combines good general light, dedicated task light, and accent light, with enough flexibility to adapt to changing requirements throughout the day.

RIGHT AND OPPOSITE During the day, when natural light levels are low, or when the kitchen is being used for purely practical purposes, the space is lit in cool white light provided by recessed downlights and the indirect lighting of the perimeter cove and central coffer, which together make up the general light in the room. (See right.) The light source for the perimeter cove and central coffer is a low-voltage xenon clickstrip, which can be dimmed from white to a warm yellow color when a cozier effect is required as natural light fades. For an energy-efficient approach, a fluorescent source could be used for daytime, switching to rope lights for an evening effect. At night, other mood settings can be employed to bring warmth and softness to the space, creating a more atmospheric ambiance conducive to dining. (See opposite.)

Table lamp

A purely atmospheric touch, this table lamp is used to add a warm yellow light that makes the space less clinical—a wonderful way to soften a hard-edged kitchen. Functional light is provided from above by the recessed downlights, which are contained in a polished stainless-steel housing fixed on the glazed roof of the projecting bay.

General light

The general light in the kitchen is created by the indirect lighting within the perimeter cove and central coffer. The light is concealed and reflects off the matte-white ceiling to provide a good level of crisp, white general light that is shadow-free. At night, the coffer is dimmed to give a soft, warmer light, and the recessed downlights provide more punch.

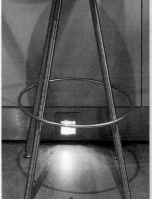

Low-level light

Introducing lighting at a low level in the toe kick adds another layering effect. This should be off during the day when the stronger general coffer lighting is at work. In the evening, when the other effects are dimmed for a relaxed mood, the recessed floor washers will come into their own, lighting the floor, and creating small pockets of light.

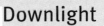

Uplight

Another element of interest and warmth has been added to the lighting scheme by installing uplights along the top of the wall units; these are used to softly uplight a collection of earthenware pots. The uplighting adds another layer of light purely for the nighttime setting, and is not used as part of the harder, brighter daytime setting.

Downlight

Within the ceiling coffers, recessed downlights are used to provide the focused task lighting on the island. The downlights focus on the ceramic objects on the suspended element in the center and on the stainless-steel sink, below. They are controlled on a circuit of their own so that, as other lights are dimmed, they can be kept brighter as a task light if desired.

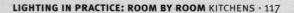

Dining areas

A dining area can be relaxed and informal, for everyday use at breakfast, lunch, and dinner, or elegant and formal, reserved for special occasions. It may be part of a kitchen or an open-plan living space, or a separate room.

Whatever the room, the key is to focus light onto the center of the table—onto the tableware or flowers—but never directly over the diners' heads. The simplest way of doing this is with one or two low-glare, low-voltage downlights with a narrow 10-degree lamp and a honeycomb louver, if necessary. A pendant or chandelier may be used as a visual focus, and some designs can be adapted to contain a downlight on a separate circuit, or a downlight can be used on either side. (See pages 76–83.) The background and accent lighting is similar to a living room. (See pages 102–107.) Each effect is controlled individually. Don't forget candles for softness and a dynamic flicker.

BELOW The opening in the wall at the end of this dining room gives a vista through to the corridor beyond. A recessed uplight set at the bottom of each shelf lights upward to create a pattern on the ceiling and contrast with the darkness of the surrounding walls. A visual focus over the dining table is provided by the large lantern. On either side of it (out of view) two small low-glare downlights with 10-deg. lamps focus on the center of the table and highlight the flowers. Creating a central focus, with candles or a narrow-beam downlight, is one of the best ways to ensure an inviting atmosphere. Small low-voltage directional downlights highlight the artworks by Jean-Marc Huss and Susan Jayne Hocking.

RIGHT Here, the pendant acts as the central focus, diffusing a soft, flattering light through its cream shade. Above the table are four discreet 10-deg. downlights that make the flatware sparkle. The still life pictures by Craig Wylie are highlighted, and the shelves are dramatically backlit. For infill general light, the uplight above the shelving can be dimmed or brightened, depending on the mood setting required.

OPPOSITE To create this intimate dining setting, the background has been left almost entirely in darkness, except for the dramatically lit picture by David Smith between the windows. This has been lit from below with a plug-in bronze highlight with a 20W 12V narrow-beam lamp with an elongating lens. It is almost more dramatic because of the contrast between the lighter parts of the painting and the background. The visual focus is the chandelier above the table, with its cream shades that cast a flattering light onto diners. Candles flicker on the table and should not be forgotten as an excellent way to add focus, movement, and softness. Around the chandelier are four dimmed low-glare narrow-beam directional downlights, with honeycomb louvers to reduce the glare further. These add a very soft light to the dining table at night, and come into their own for lunch parties in this dark room, creating sparkle and adding interest.

ABOVE Even in country kitchens, being able to control the lights appropriately can create areas of intimacy. Here, when the rest of the lights are dimmed, the discreet narrow-focus surface spots located in the beams above the table accentuate the dining area and make this room within a room an inviting draw.

RIGHT This chainmail chandelier over a table creates an intimate dining area and echoes the chainmail hanging in the window behind. This is the type of chandelier into which a central spotlight could be introduced on a separate circuit to create more drama on the table in the evening. (See page 79.)

Top tips for dining rooms

Install a couple of narrow-beam lights over the dining table to provide a soft, atmospheric glow in its center. Dimmed downlights, highlighting the crystal and flatware, create a stunning effect.

If you have a central crystal chandelier, ensure that it is on its own switch so that it can be dimmed to a decorative glow. Then add two discreet downlights on either side, which will make the crystal sparkle as if it is internally lit.

Decide what the focal points are and light them. It may simply be the curtains, which should be lit with low-voltage downlights, or an alcove or recess, which can be uplit to create a dramatic feature.

Dining rooms often have other uses. If you are planning to use the room as a study or home office as well, make sure that you have adequate lighting for reading and working. A freestanding uplight can often provide the solution for the secondary task.

Bedrooms

A private retreat and a place for relaxation and sleep, a bedroom needs to be bright in the morning to engender that "get up and go" feeling, and intimate and atmospheric at night to promote rest.

The aim in a bedroom is to achieve a soft background light without glare. In rooms that are large enough to accommodate freestanding furniture, this practical general lighting is often best provided by lamps. This lighting would always be controlled separately from the bedside lights. Where space is limited and in contemporary interiors, an uplighting solution can be appropriate on one side of the room, perhaps creating a cove. If there are closets, their doors can be wall-washed with recessed downlights. Sometimes low-glare downlights can be used to highlight an extravagant headboard, creating focus in the room. This can work well, but remember to control these on a separate switch so they can be turned off at bedtime to avoid direct glare.

Taking inspiration from five-star hotels, additional low-level light can be introduced, such as recessed floor washers by the entrance to the bathroom or under a bedside table. The bed can have a rope light below it, to create a floating effect. This type of light is especially effective as a night-light.

Bedroom task lighting is usually associated with reading in bed. If this is to be achieved with a table lamp or wall light, the bottom of the shade needs to be about shoulder height to provide a spread of light over the page. Any lower and the light will be cast too low; too high and you will get glare from the bulb. A swing-arm wall light

LEFT This large country bedroom is softly lit by the bedside lamps and the floor lamp behind the sofa. The effect from the floor lamp is far softer because of the translucent shade, as opposed to the opaque shades on the bedside lights that create a definite up-and-down light. As there is no side lighting, another light source is provided in the form of a slim LED reading light. A few architectural features finish the look—a small recessed uplight illuminates the center of the window arch behind the floor lamp. Some discreet bronze low-voltage spots are concealed between the beams to highlight features such as the picture to the left of the bed and the blue vase on the low table between the seating arrangement.

RIGHT This contemporary four-poster bed has no overhead canopy and only small side tables. Instead of the expected table lamps, two pendants hover above each side table, providing a soft glow and keeping the table free for books or other objects. The pendants are purely decorative, so the two slim adjustable fiber-optic reading lights provide just enough light to cover the page and not disturb your partner. The Japanese lacquered panels of cherry blossom above the bed are softly lit by two directional lights in the ceiling above. These are directed toward the panels and are on a separate circuit so that they can be switched off at bedtime.

ABOVE The visual reference of light in this children's room is the table lamp between the two beds. The room is divided into two by a simple screen, with the beds set against it on one side and bookcases on the other. The screen conceals uplights that create a soft glow across the beamed ceiling. Unobtrusively hidden from direct view is the contemporary effect of small downlights between the beams. One on each side focuses on the pillows providing good reading light. Others add infill light, catching the beanbags and games table.

Top tips for bedrooms

Light the front of closets with discreet low-voltage downlights. This adds a practical light source, as well as increasing general light.

Localized lamps provide the best sort of background lighting for a bedroom, ideally one positioned on either side of the bed, plus one or two others.

A bedside reading lamp may be sufficient for reading, but a fiber-optic light or LED provides a focused light—just right for the pages of a book.

LEFT This bedroom features wonderful Lalique pieces displayed in the horizontal niches. The lighting has been achieved with tiny fiber optics that focus on each intricate glass sculpture so that the light seems trapped within, and they glow like jewels.

BELOW LEFT The general light in this simple guest room is provided by a chandelier (out of view), but the two wall lights with adjustable arms, positioned over both sides of the bed, add light for reading and keep the small side tables clear. The key with a bedside wall light is to ensure the bottom of the shade is just above shoulder height. When a person is sitting in bed, light is cast over the page. If it is too low it misses; too high and it can cause glare.

BELOW This country bedroom has two lamps framing the bed, the translucent shades providing a soft sideways light. The shade is at a good height, as the fall of light comes neatly over each side of the bed as task lighting. Above are two reading spotlights, which offer an individual focus for over a book for each person, allowing the other to sleep undisturbed.

follows similar rules in positioning, but can be a more practical option as you can adjust it as required.

The pendant is another form of bedside light that has become fashionable, particularly when used in a restricted area because it avoids the clutter of a lamp on the bedside table. For positioning, follow the same rules for the shade on a table lamp. It is usually more of a decorative effect than an adequate reading light.

Perhaps the most practical solution, which can be used to supplement a bedside lamp or pendant, is a flexible LED wall light inspired by the old first-class seats in planes. Similar to a torch light, localized light is focused on the page with little spill to disturb your partner. It can be wall-mounted or fixed to the headboard.

RIGHT This theatrical, almost Empire-style room has two obvious light effects. The dramatic urns flanking the bed are backlit, adding atmosphere but inadequate reading light. A solution is offered by individual task lights with an LED source mounted on either side of the headboard.

BELOW LEFT A simple table lamp provides task lighting at the correct level for reading in bed, as well as for when sitting at the table. The glass base is unobtrusive in this pale cream bedroom, and the off-white shade diffuses a soft light.

FAR RIGHT This wonderful ceiling of stars above a child's bed is more for decorative effect than for giving much light. It is created by miniature fiber optics piercing the ceiling in a random pattern, just like stars in the sky. The installation is most easily achieved with access from above. When dimmed, the 35W 12V low-voltage light source can be left on as a night-light. Color wheels and flicker wheels can be incorporated within the remote fiber-optic box.

TOP RIGHT Here, light has been introduced to a closet by an LED light source incorporated within the clothes rail, which lights up all the garments.

BELOW LEFT This narrow dressing area is half open and half closed. The neat rectangular ceiling fixtures contain two directional downlights that light in both directions from the single fixture. Two downlights may have seemed too cluttered in this space. Directing light toward the closet means that it is not necessary to introduce internal fixtures.

FAR RIGHT At the end of this changing area, which has built-in cabinets along one side, is a mirror. Creating the ideal light for a dressing area such as this is tricky. Overhead downlights alone would have been unflattering, so they are directed sideways to the cabinets, usefully lighting the contents when the doors are opened and reflecting off of them when they are closed. The frosted square lights recessed into the mirror provide a flattering, soft light to anyone standing in front of the mirror.

In certain situations, usually when there is a low ceiling, some people prefer a narrow-beam low-glare spotlight that can be operated independently. The key is to position this skillfully to avoid glare off of a page.

Dressing areas can be part of the bedroom or a stand-alone room. In the bedroom, directing light toward the closet, either with a concealed strip or a directional downlight, can be effective, as this lights the interior when the closet doors are opened and adds a soft reflected light to the room when they are closed.

There are various solutions for inside the closet. One of the most popular, but also one of the most expensive, solutions is the clothes rail with integrated lighting (usually a white LED source). This looks good, but is not as effective as the tried-and-tested method of a strip light behind a pelmet, which gives a more even light to the front of the hanging clothes. Another trick is to have a strip at the back of a shelf above a clothes rail, casting lighting up and down. Lighting closets can almost reach retail levels—for example, shoe niches can be individually lit with tiny LEDs.

These types of information light can be controlled by a door-operated switch, which is effective as long as the doors are closed, but will stay on if they are left open. The other solution is a presence detector with a small sensor in the ceiling of the closet. The light comes on when you stand in front of the closet and goes off after a while when you leave the area.

In stand-alone dressing rooms, it is important to introduce an element of indirect light. This is often best achieved by uplighting from the top of the cabinets, as long as there is at least 6–8 inches (150–200mm) above them. If the dressing room leads from the bedroom to the bathroom, a low-level night-light can be useful, especially one on a presence detector.

SPOTLIGHT ON a comfortable, generously sized contemporary bedroom. Several lighting effects work together to create a warm, soothing mood and bring out the best in the sumptuous materials used. The striking feature of the room is the backlit headboard.

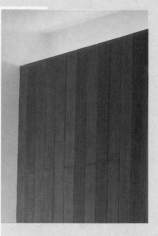

Bedside lamp

This shows the visual focus of light—what you expect to see by each bedside. In many instances, the bedside lamp also acts as a task light, providing adequate light for reading. The crucial factor is the choice of shade and its height—the lower edge should be at shoulder height when a person is sitting in bed. This is often difficult to achieve, as sometimes it can be awkward to position the lamp close enough to the bed. The table lamps in this bedroom are just for visual effect and to create a glow.

Accent lighting

This is an unusual but stunning effect. The headboard is raised off of the back wall, and a soft light is concealed behind it to achieve a halo effect. This is not for use during the daytime, but can be switched on in the evening and even used as a night-light. A suitable light source for this type of effect is lightstream, a flexible rope-style fitting that needs to be completely concealed from view. The headboard will need to be about 1¾ in. (40mm) from the wall for this to be successful.

Task lighting

A small LED reading light has been recessed into the side of the headboard. With its own switch, it is totally independent of the other lighting within the room. It has a 1.2W bulb and a focused beam that will light only the page of a book, making it an ideal bedside task light. A reading light such as this can be fixed either to the headboard, as it is here, or to the wall.

Downlight

Rectangular downlights are used to provide infill lighting in the center of this large room. One is used to catch the throw at the end of the bed, and those at the other end of the room light the floor and seating (out of view). They help as accent lighting and prevent the center of the room from being dark. It would have been difficult to add additional lamp light in this area and keep it clutter-free. It is important with downlights over beds that they are controlled on their own circuit so that they can be turned off when you are lying in bed.

Uplight

Along the wall at the entrance of the bedroom is a wood wall, which conceals the air-conditioning grilles. Lowering this section of wall and concealing a light source above is a good way of introducing a general background light with uplight. Two different light sources could be used to achieve this effect—an overlapping fluorescent for daytime or when bright light is needed, changing to a soft lightstream or warm LED strip for an evening effect when only a warm glow is required.

OPPOSITE This dramatic contemporary bedroom is a good example of how lighting can be used to create emphasis. It features a balanced combination of cleverly concealed background light, effective task lighting, and soft accent lighting. Each effect, described in detail above, being controlled individually to create maximum impact.

Bathrooms

Sometimes the bathroom needs to have a spalike quality, making it the ultimate sanctuary for relaxing, bathing, and pampering. At other times, usually in the morning, it needs to be bright, fresh, and practical, with a good flattering light at the mirror for putting on makeup and shaving.

Bathrooms respond well to light, as the materials used there are usually reflective. Good lighting can make a tiny bathroom seem bigger and a large bathroom feel more intimate. When planning lighting for a generous-size bathroom, the best approach is to treat the space as you would any other room, and create different layers of lighting effects. On a practical level, there are various zones applied to bathrooms defined by how close they are to the wet areas. In an around tubs and showers use light fixtures that are rated for wet areas. Because traditional decorative fixtures intended for use in bathrooms need to be sealed to meet these requirements, manufacturers have developed solutions where the light source is sealed, but can still have a shade.

The general light in a bathroom is usually provided by recessed downlights, which reflect well off of stone and tiled surfaces. The positioning of these is key, as they can provide a harsh and unflattering light for the face when badly located. Where possible, downlights are best concealed. For example, if a recessed slot can be created against the back wall of a bathtub or shower, then the light source can be concealed within this and the light effect will streak down the wall, almost like running water. When installing such lights, it is essential to consider how they are set out, as they need to be centered on the tiles or panels. This is not the best lighting solution if mosaic tiles have been used, as a close offset light will emphasize the grout lines and show up any imperfections. In this case, recessed downlights

OPPOSITE This luxurious dark marble bathroom is dramatically lit. Downlights focus along the length of the vanity, and on either side fluorescent strip lights are located behind narrow panels of frosted glass to create a good facial light. These are practical, but should be switched off for the atmospheric mood settings. The shower has a large niche accented by two waterproof low-glare 20W 12V downlights. At low level, three floor washers on either side of the shower are concealed beneath the marble bench, and streak light across the shower tray.

LEFT On the back wall of this contemporary shower cubicle in a period interior are waterproof 12V lights—a useful solution when lights cannot be recessed into a high or period ceiling.

ABOVE The general light from recessed downlights is softened by the concealed uplight above the shower and closet doors. Without this, the light is sharp and hard. It was important to introduce light in different directions to create a balanced effect. Two shower lights have been set into a slot in the back wall of the shower so that the light seems to stream down the wall like running water.

pulled out from the wall to give a soft wall wash will be more effective. If the ceiling is very high, light fixtures do not need to be recessed; instead, waterproof surface fixtures can be used, positioned just above tiling level. (See page 130, left.) General light can also be provided by a chandelier or by uplighting—along the top of a mirror or cabinet, for example, or by creating a coffer in the ceiling—which provides an even, diffuse light.

The next effect to be considered is the task lighting that will light the mirror and face. A single downlight will create really unbecoming shadows and should be avoided. Two are far better, as you can stand between them and, as long as the sink or vanity is white or light in color, the reflected light will help to fill in the downlight effect. This is not the ideal solution, but in certain situations where a very clean look is required it can be the only option. A single downlight, to create sparkle, can be acceptable if there are lights mounted on either side of the mirror, as this is the most flattering light for the face.

To create a flattering light, it is essential to ensure a shadow-free situation on both sides of the mirror, and this is best achieved with a light source on each side. These can either be mounted within the mirror or be separate from it. In a traditional setting, decorative wall lights may be an appealing option. In contemporary bathrooms where a cleaner, crisper look is required, concealing the light with frosted glass behind the mirror can be an effective solution. (See pages 131 and 135.) For a bright light, a fluorescent source in a warm white color is probably the best choice. Ideally, this should be dimmable, but should definitely be controlled separately from the other lighting in the room. If a softer light is required, then a tungsten tube may be the answer, but this produces less light and is less energy efficient with a higher maintenance factor. Another way to create side light is to set a small mirror within a recess and backlight it so that the light bounces off the side walls, providing a soft indirect light. (See page 69.)

LEFT This bathroom has such a high ceiling that it is safe to incorporate a decorative chandelier above the tub. This creates a glamorous contrast to the brick wall.

OPPOSITE The focal point here is the theatrical tub, with a niche at the end lit by two recessed uplights with 20W 12V 20-deg. lamps. Reflected in the mirror are two lamps that use low-voltage bulbs, and are hard-wired to meet regulations.

"Bathrooms should be places where well-considered lighting brings out the best in all the materials used, and lighting control really makes a space work to create different moods."

BELOW This detail of a double sink illustrates three layers of lighting effects. Downlights are used to light the limestone sinks and surface from above. The recessed wood niche is also lit from above using shallow low-voltage 20W 12V sealed undercabinet lights, to create interest and highlight the objects. Finally, an LED strip is used under the sink unit and dimmed to give a soft glow that is also useful as a night-light.

BELOW RIGHT The expanse of mirror makes the space seem twice the size, and introducing any side light would have compromised the scheme. Hence a recess was developed at the top of the mirror, concealed with frosted glass, that allows a warm fluorescent strip to soften the effect of the downlights and minimize harsh shadows on the face. Below the vanity unit, a line of warm white LEDs has been used. This is off when all the other lights are on full and comes into its own as a layering effect on the moodier settings.

OPPOSITE Here, the vanity and mirror are two distinct blocks. These are made to "float" by incorporating a xenon clickstrip (or warm white LED strip) below each unit. One lights the floor, while the other gives a soft glow to the vanity itself. For facial lighting, the two side panels of the mirror have become light boxes, with a concealed warm white fluorescent source. It is always an advantage to be able to dim fluorescent light, otherwise it can only be used on the brightest setting, which will kill all other mood settings as its brightness is greater than any of the other sources.

To introduce layers of light into a bathroom, use light effects at different levels. Light niches to create small pockets of light, use recessed lights under a bath plinth, uplight an architectural detail or position low-level floor washers under a vanity or recess them into the wall to give a soft glow on the floor. This low-level feature lighting is also useful as a night-light. Each effect can be dramatic, or dimmed to create a candlelight experience, and will help to build up the overall mood of the room.

Usually three switch lines are required, each one controlled individually and ideally dimmable. If three switches or dimmers seem too confusing, the night-light mood circuit could operate on a presence detector (PIR) linked back to a rotary dimmer located remotely to preset the night-light level. This is particularly effective in children's bathrooms.

The downstairs cloakroom should not be forgotten. Use all the same tricks. Provide good lighting for the face, and add another layer of lighting in the form of a lit niche behind the lavatory, or introduce low-level floor washers and create a floating effect under the sink.

Top tips for bathrooms

Task lighting is important at the mirror, where you need to see clearly for shaving and applying makeup. The most flattering way to achieve this is to light from both sides so that the face is illuminated evenly.

Don't forget to pay attention to the shower area. An effective feature is to position downlights close to the back wall, ideally in a slot, to create a dramatic shaft of light. This is not a good solution if the shower wall is mosaic or the grouting is less than perfect, as it will highlight any and all imperfections.

Ensure that all lighting used is specifically designed for the bathroom. Check that the IP rating of the fixture is appropriate to the zone in which it is to be located.

Think about feature lighting to create atmosphere. Put recessed spots into alcoves; backlight an opaque bathtub panel, which could even change color as a result; uplight behind the bathtub with waterproof uplights; or use a floor washer as a night-light or to create a glow under a vanity.

The lighting should be controlled on at least two different switch lines. Ideally, dim the lighting to help create different moods or use a preset system so that the mood changes instantly, providing different settings for day, early evening, and late at night.

SPOTLIGHT ON an expansive and supremely relaxing bathroom. It is decorated in warm, pale tones of cream, which reflect the light and make the room seem bright and airy.

RIGHT AND OPPOSITE This wonderful, spacious bathroom has the feel of a serene living room, with a pleasing contrast between the crisp contemporary lines of the architecture and built-in units, and the antique chair and bowl. This bathroom illustrates the value of layered lighting, with infill general light from recessed low-glare downlights, task lighting on either side of the mirror that infills the center, and at low level, the soft glow that makes the cabinets appear to float.

Downlight

The tub is lit from above with a 35W 12V narrow-beam downlight, creating a glow of reflected light on the ceramic surface. To avoid glare to the bather, a 10–14-deg. lamp with a honeycomb louver should be used. It also provides a good solution for reading in the tub. This circuit should be controlled individually, so that it can be turned off for the relaxing setting.

Low-level light

The floating effect created by the floor washers in the vanity's toe-kick area is not for use during the day, but is part of the softer evening settings, then used as a night-light. Xenon is a possible source for this effect, but beware of too many reflections of the light source. Warm white LED strips can also be used to achieve this effect if the floor is polished.

Task lighting

This task mirror has a magnifying glass, and the built-in light works well for illuminating the face. This is a particularly good solution when the layout of the room makes it difficult to incorporate a standard mirror—for example, when a lav is located in front of a window, such as in an attic bathroom where the sink is fitted into a dormer window.

Side lighting

The most flattering light is provided by light boxes on each side of the mirror, created by concealing the sources behind frosted-glass strips. The light boxes need to be a minimum of 3¼ in. (80mm) deep so that there is no direct imaging of the light sources. Various sources are possible— xenon for a soft, warm light, and fluorescent for a sharper, brighter light.

Downlight

The small recessed downlight is the most commonly used lighting tool in bathrooms. The discreet halogen downlight responds well to tiled, marble, and ceramic surfaces, creating a sparkle and highlight that no energy-efficient fluorescent downlight can achieve. Bear in mind that, when overhead, it can cast unflattering shadows.

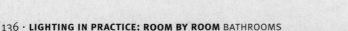

Using an attic area as a home office is an excellent use of space. Here, the desk is suspended across the window, which fills the space with natural light during the day. At dusk, the desk lamps provide working light at close quarters, but the clever low bookcases on either side of the room have overlapping fluorescents concealed under a white frosted-glass panel on top. These flood the whole area with a soft, bright, white light, creating ideal background illumination for a home office. In a children's room, a second line of fluorescents could be used with a colored sleeve to introduce a fun element.

Working areas

Always essential for a home office or study area is a good dedicated task light for close desk work. (See pages 72–75.) How you light the rest of the room will depend on the type of space and how much natural light it receives.

A work space within the home may mean a fully functioning office located in a spare room, attic, basement, or even an outbuilding in the garden. It may be a study or library, or simply a desk in a corner of the living room or kitchen, or tucked away on a landing or hallway. Wherever it is and whatever form it takes, what is crucial is to create the right environment in which to work.

The first factor to consider is the background lighting. This is best achieved indirectly in a work space, by light reflected off the ceiling or walls from uplights, downlights, or concealed lighting.

Top tips for attic spaces

Traditionally used for deep storage, many attics have now been reclaimed within houses and used as additional bedrooms, children's play areas, media rooms, or home offices. The awkward shape of a pitched roof makes these spaces problematic to light, as the ceiling is usually high at the center of the room, but drops under the slope toward the edges.

If there are central beams overhead, these can be used for uplighting. Low-voltage surface spotlights with a remote transformer, preferably color matched to the beam (use bronze or black fixtures on dark beams and brushed aluminum on light beams), should be mounted on either side ideally not project below the beam for the most unobtrusive effect.

Install receptacles at a low level in the corners and along the sides of the room for plug-in solutions, such as low-level uplights or contemporary illuminated side tables or sculptural lights. (See page 166.) These come in a variety of shapes and sizes, and can be very effective, sending soft light in all directions.

Another solution, if the pitch is high enough, is to stretch a low-voltage wire system from one side of the room to the other. Ideally, the transformer would be located remotely—it should be within 10 ft. (3m) of the beginning of the cable, and the distance of the cable should not be longer than 20 ft. (6m), as otherwise a voltage drop will be visible. Spotlights designed for the wire system can then be located at any position where light is required.

Top tips for home offices

Ensure that there is a good level of background lighting in the room. This could be uplighting from bookcases or a cupboard, or a wall-wash effect.

Always incorporate a dedicated task light so that the light level can be increased for detailed desk work.

Make sure that the task lighting is controlled independently from the rest of the lighting, particularly if the home office is within an open-plan space. This will allow the rest of the lighting to be dimmed for television viewing, for example, while the desk area is still kept bright.

If the "home office" or desk area is usually concealed within a cabinet, ensure that task lighting is built into the shelves above. The lighting should be locally dimmable so that the right level can be set for work and for when it is not in use to contribute to the feature lighting.

ABOVE This dark paneled library uses only traditional light sources to create ambiance, in keeping with the style of the interior. The background lighting in the room is provided by the overhead chandelier. Wall lights frame the fireplace, giving a midlevel glow, and the adjustable Anglepoise® lamp on the desk provides the task light.

RIGHT This working area is tucked into one end of a bedroom. On the wall behind the desk is a recess at ceiling level, which conceals a line of fluorescent tubing that also lights the painting, *Poème caché* by Claude le Boul. Although a warm-colored lamp is used, at night it gives a feeling of daylight filtering through, providing a soft, diffuse light that is ideal for working. The table lamp gives a warm glow and provides an element of task lighting, but is more in keeping with the feeling of the bedroom than conventional task lighting.

Secondly, and probably the most important factor for a home office, is the task lighting, which, in its simplest form is a desk lamp. In the past, these fixtures usually had tungsten incandescent bulbs, but these days there is an ever-increasing range that use fluorescent or compact light sources. These are far more effective to sit under for long periods of time, as they are much cooler and provide a far more even light.

Sometimes, where space is restricted, the home office is squeezed into a corner of the room within a self-contained storage unit, perhaps with a pullout desk. Uplighting from the top shelf of such a unit can be used to provide indirect light, while some undercupboard lighting below the lowest shelf provides the task light.

BELOW Out of view in this dedicated home office there is a diffuse general light created by fluorescent uplighting above the bookcase and small directional 50W 12V halogen downlights with 27-deg. medium-beam lamps, providing a soft wash of light on the working surface. The lamp creates an area of light at a local level. Beyond the window, the small terrace has a focused spot of light on the box topiary balls and creates an interesting vista to enjoy at night, increasing the feeling of space, rather than one of dark closed blinds.

Halls, corridors, stairs, and landings

These are often the forgotten areas in the home, the last to be considered, and the ones with the bare lightbulb or boring paper lantern hanging rather bleakly. But with a little creative thought and planning, they are actually the areas in which you can have the most fun with lighting.

These are the passageways of a home, the spaces in which you never really linger. Yet these "roads" also link all of the rooms, so they should not be forgotten. Imagine walking from an atmospheric dining room into a stark, bright hall on the way to a living room—the mood would be lost. The hall should set the scene, creating a seamless transition from one space to the next.

These spaces can be difficult to tackle, as their proportions are often compromised—they may appear too narrow, too tall, or too low—but there are several solutions. A row of central downlights is usually best avoided, unless they are to be directed toward the wall. The layering techniques used in larger rooms should also be applied to these spaces. In a traditional narrow hallway, for example, a large lantern can set the tone—overscaling is always effective. It should be dimmable to avoid glare from the light source. Add some downlights to provide more infill light, and use these to light artwork on the wall. In addition, you can use low-level floor washers set into the wall at about 8 inches (200mm) above the floor, with a concealed asymmetric source that lights the floor. This, together with the dropped lantern, will help to adjust the tall, narrow scale of the hall, and provide a focus on the floor. The next trick is to light something beyond, such as a picture or, if there is a staircase, an object on the landing. This helps to direct the focus and draw you through the space.

In a low-ceilinged contemporary interior, other tricks come into play. In a passage too narrow for wall lights, recessed slots can be created in the wall that can be uplit or downlit, or both. This produces dramatic shafts of light, with pools of light on the ceiling or floor, or both. The advantage is a dramatic effect with nothing protruding into the corridor. (See page 144.)

One way to make a very long hall seem shorter is to create a series of "rooms" along the passage that are treated in different ways. This is easier to achieve if the interior design can change as well, to emphasize the zones. For example, light the first part of a passage with only low-level floor washers. Use downlights to illuminate artwork, and a recessed coffer in the ceiling to create a soft, diffuse light. At the far end, recessed uplights can be added to emphasize a wonderful texture on a wall. Not all of this may be possible, but the key is to be brave and exaggerate effects for maximum impact.

ABOVE In most corridors, it is best to avoid using a simple line of downlights because walking under them is always slightly uncomfortable, particularly if the ceiling is low. In this corridor, asymmetry works well, with the offset directional low-voltage downlights lighting the silvered panels on the right. The recessed square low-voltage floor washers on the left light the floor and throw light across to the other side. In addition, the wonderful line of torchière wall lights, created out of bronze "twigs," uplight the ceiling, creating unusual shadows.

OPPOSITE LEFT Scale is always important. This narrow corridor in a period town house has an extremely high ceiling. The large lanterns hang down and fill the volume, effectively seeming to reduce the height of the ceiling. The lower part of the space would have remained

unlit, however, so square recessed 20W 12V floor washers were used to highlight the floor. Both light effects can be balanced at different times of the day to change the emphasis and create different impacts.

ABOVE RIGHT This view from a hall to a guest bathroom is made interesting by the variety of lighting effects. In the foreground, a wonderfully crafted wall light sends a soft, diffuse light through the orange shade, and also creates an up-and-downlight effect. Beyond, general light is indirect, from the recessed uplights in the central ceiling coffer, while downlights are located in the recessed zone for hanging coats.

"Create drama by using an overscaled decorative pendant, dimmed for mood, combined with downlights that actually create the effect, whether spotlighting a picture or highlighting flowers."

Stairs can be regarded as a sculpture within the house and should be celebrated. Lighting is essential, especially from a safety point of view, although it should not stop there. The availability of discreet light sources means that there are endless possibilities. Individual stair lights could be used on every tread or on every other, and there are many suitable low-energy LED fixtures. A glass staircase can be uplit from below or have lights integrated into the treads. Recessed downlights under a sloping soffit should be avoided, as they will shine in your eyes. An up-and-downlight can be used in the corner of a narrow staircase to send light down onto the steps and to uplight the underside of the sloping soffit of the stair above.

The underside of stairs is often overlooked, but if left open, it can be made into a feature through clever lighting. In a modern setting, recessed uplights could be used, while in a traditional interior, suitable solutions are a freestanding uplight plugged in behind a log basket or or a lamp on a low chest. Lighting under a staircase in a narrow hall will draw that area into the hall, and make the whole space feel wider. (See page 58.)

LEFT This long corridor is broken up by the variety of lighting effects that help to focus the attention and create interest. First, on the left are the seven dramatic niches. These are uplit at the bottom with a 20W 12V low-heat uplight, creating a wonderful play of light and shadow. (See also page 118.) The niches appear almost like recessed wall lights, lit along their length, with the light escaping at the top and creating a pattern on the ceiling. A similar pattern could be achieved on the floor if downlights were used. This play of shadows is continued with pools of light along the floor from downlights, some directed toward the wall to light the artwork. In the hall at the end of the corridor, wall lamps frame the entrance door and provide visual focus.

OPPOSITE TOP This unusual basement corridor in a historic building has shallow archways, which have been uplit with 20W 12V uplights. The effect of the light catching each arch helps to visually foreshorten the length of the corridor. On the sideboard are two candle lamps that provide a decorative mid-layer of light. Discreet downlights between the arches create pools of light along the length of the corridor, leading to the visual impact of the bust in the niche at the end. Each effect is controlled individually, to create the perfect balance of light and shadow at different times of the day.

OPPOSITE BOTTOM LEFT This open-tread glass staircase is lit from below with low-heat 20W 12V uplights. The beam is narrow, and the light sources shine upward

Top tips for halls and stairs

Don't worry about symmetry—lighting can be dramatic. Use recessed downlights on one side of a hall to create a wall wash in combination with recessed floor washers, to provide an interesting low-level contrast.

Draw the eye to the next spot by lighting something beyond, such as on the half-landing of a stairway—this could be an object, a picture, or a view beyond a window.

Use shallow wall lights or table lights to create a soft glow. Up-and-downlights are particularly effective in a narrow hallway.

Always remember to dim the hallway lighting. It is a false economy not to when all the other areas leading off it can be dimmed.

Stairs can be an interesting architectural feature, which can be enhanced with individual stair lights. A low-level floor washer on every third step works well when it is not possible to recess fixtures into the sloping ceiling above.

Light the half-landing at the top of the stairs with a decorative fixture to provide interest and drama. A slim up-and-downlight that will not project into the stairwell is ideal at the corners.

Use recessed uplights to highlight architectural features on the stairs, such as a window or arch.

A chandelier or dramatic pendant can be hung over the center of a large staircase to provide both a visual focus and light.

onto the frosted-glass stair treads. This is a useful and effective way to light stairs, because each tread retains a glow from the light.

FAR RIGHT These stairs are lit with square 20W 12V floor washers. Lighting stairs in such a way is useful when there is little option for other light sources—for example, if the ceiling above is sloping or if the stairs are too narrow to use wall lights. When recessed washers are used, if the spread is wide enough, they can be positioned to light every third tread. Alternatively, use them to light every other tread, as here, and then a pattern of light and shadow will define the steps. Another option is to light every step with an indicator light, using a small LED light source directed at an angle, which means there is no glare.

Pathways, exteriors, and entrances

The first impression of a house is its approach, which sets the tone for what is to come. At night, the lighting outside the entrance plays a major role in determining the mood and engendering feelings of welcome and hospitality.

ABOVE This welcoming entrance is defined by the lighting. The wall lights have mesh over the top of the fixture to give a soft glow and a sharp downlight effect for drama. They frame the window on the wall leading up to the front door, and flank the entrance itself. The effect also throws the box topiary balls and tree into silhouette. The entrance arch defines the porch, where two downlights focus on the threshold. The enticing glow inside invites you, with the strong focus of the low-voltage spotlight on the circular artwork.

If the only light at an entrance is a security light, not only is it unfriendly and glaring, but also it makes visitors feel like trespassers. Framing the door with two wall lights, traditional or modern, or an overhead lantern—ideally slightly dimmed to take the edge off the glare—makes a far more welcoming approach. In a country setting, without the additional lighting from surrounding streets, this may not provide enough light. In this case, a soft uplight to planting, filtering dappled light across the sides of the building, will soften the starkness of the effect, although it will still appear as if the wall lights are doing

LEFT The entrance to this town house is not lit with two lanterns, as expected, but there is a drama of layered light and a play of light and shadow, as each of the architectural elements is accentuated. The stairs are lit by square recessed fixtures on each side. The door is framed with low-glare low-voltage uplights that catch on the opening and molding above to dramatic effect, providing the perfect welcome. The lights can be controlled by an internal dimmer switch, if they are to be left on to welcome a visitor. On a day-to-day basis, however, they operate on a motion sensor, providing enough light for opening the door.

BELOW This wonderful chateau stands in the middle of the French countryside, so a little light goes a long way. The light grazes up the walls, emphasizing the texture of the stone and catching the edges of the windowsills. Despite the scale of the building, only 35W 12V uplights were used, which make a significant impact on the wall. The reflected light from this effect also provides ambient lighting for the courtyard beyond.

the work. Lighting the side of a building is a good way of creating general illumination. Another way of emphasizing an entrance, when wall lights are inappropriate, is with recessed uplights close to the architrave of the door. Another option is to uplight a pair of plants either side.

Having established the lighting of the entrance, the next thing to think of is the approach. Lighting stairs is important for safety. If the stairs have sides, then a discreet light can be set into the wall to skim across each stair. Achieve this using a fixture with the lamp set deeply within it, and either an LED or low-voltage halogen light source with a lens to direct the light and ensure minimal glare. Another way to light steps is with spiked spotlights. (See page 148.) Once again, the best results are achieved when the light source is concealed, either by the surrounding planting or by using a fitting in which the lamp is set well back.

Floodlighting an exterior can be a way of enhancing an approach, also creating reflected light to illuminate a terrace. Avoid the standard approach of floodlights offset from the building by several feet and directed toward it, as not only will this create glare affecting anyone looking out of the building, but it will also flatten any architectural

Top tips for entrances and exteriors

Uplight the facade of a building through planting, as this softens the effect, and sends soft shadows up the face of the building, for a subtle and gentle feel.

Emphasize the main architectural features of the entrance, just as you would indoors, with close-set uplights.

Remember to light stairs or any change of level, which would otherwise become a tripping hazard. The general rule with outside lighting is to create focal points at intervals along a path, and not necessarily to light the whole path. Again, always light a change in level or a set of stairs.

One of the golden rules of lighting, "What is left unlit is as important as what is lit," is never more true than in a garden. Lighting every tree along a driveway may be too much, but creating focus on a single tree can be magical.

Use low-level lights to provide a wash of light over a pathway. For example, a "footlighter," which is shaped like a shallow Chinese hat, positioned about 12 in. (30cm) from the path, will give a soft light all around, including over lawn or low scrubs. Or use a more specific indicator light at a low level on the path to create concentrated pools of light. If there are low bushes or hedges, hiding a light within them, to project out just above, can be effective and discreet, particularly if the fixture is a dark green color that blends in with the shrubbery.

Lighting a tree 26–39 ft. (8–12m) above the ground results in a dappled light known as "moonlighting." The light source must be heavily shielded so that it is not easily visible. Possible sources are a metal-halide, which has a slightly blue color, or a low-voltage 35W 12V copper halogen spot for a softer effect.

details—whether a column, window surround, or old textured stone facade. A subtle balance is required, because if the lighting is too close to the building it will emphasize any imperfections on the surface. Any light set into the ground will need some form of glare shielding, usually a honeycomb filter or a louver.

It is not essential to light paths uniformly, but usually just at changes of directions or every 33–50 feet (10–15m). Shielded fixtures set 16–24 inches (400–600mm) above the ground with the light directed toward the path are ideal. The light may be those set in one direction or the old-fashioned mushroom lights, which provide a soft 360-degree light over all surrounding low-level planting and the pathway. In each case, both the light source and the light fixture should be concealed among planting. If there are no plants, other solutions can be explored, such as setting light into a large stone ball to graze against the gravel, or selecting a large freestanding floor lantern and concealing a light source at the top so that the light floods out across the path.

ABOVE Lighting stairs in a garden can be difficult, but is a necessity for reasons of safety, particularly at night. One solution is to set the lights, such as small low-glare LEDs, into the side wall, if there is one. If this is not possible, as here, small exterior spotlights—again with the light source recessed and a glare guard—can be used to skim light across each step close to the riser, and create pools of light on the planting opposite.

OPPOSITE This wonderful townhouse garden has areas of focus, with a sculptural element at the end of the garden. It plays with asymmetry and materials, with the high trees to the left and the low lawn to the

right, and the stone path changing to decking at the seating area. Each effect is emphasized individually by the lighting. The trees are uplit from the low planting below, and the light reflects off the delicate branches, creating a wonderful effect. The striking sculpture at the end of the pathway is lit by a spiked spotlight tucked into the planting to the left. Lighting a sculpture from one side is effective. It creates more shadow, whereas lighting it from both ways would have flattened its texture. On the right, a small box fixture at the edge of the path creates a dramatic lighting effect in both directions, skimming across the path and the well-manicured lawn, and lighting a yew hedge beyond (out of view) on the right.

Outdoor entertaining

Whether the outside dining space is a roof terrace, balcony, or a small garden, it should be treated as another room. Not only does it provide an additional entertaining area, but it can also extend the feeling of space inside by creating a view beyond.

The trick with lighting the outside is to avoid the "black hole" effect. This is a key factor when lighting a conservatory, too, which comes alive if the garden beyond it is also lit. As ever, the first thing to decide is what to light. If the garden is surrounded by trellis, then lighting can be discreetly located at a high level to direct light downward, which can increase the general light levels, as well as adding another layer to the lighting effects—especially when combined with uplighting. The seating area or dining table is usually the central focus. If the building is high or if there is a tall tree, concealing a light at a high level to focus a narrow pool of light on a coffee or dining table, in a similar way as you would indoors, can sometimes work well. This will be effective only if the spotlight is high enough and the light source is concealed with a glare cowl. The light should only be tilted by 15–20 degrees to achieve the desired effect—any more and it is likely to cause glare.

Uplighting planting is the obvious way to add interest in an outdoor space, but the right type of planting is needed to achieve the best effect. Open foliage such as that of a laurel tree or olive tree is ideal, while a tighter clipped tree can also be lit like a sculpture by a spotlight located at a small distance. Low box topiary balls are impossible to uplight, but can be downlit to good effect or put into silhouette, especially if they frame the entrance to a home. Spiked lighting with low-voltage light sources and a remote transformer offers flexible solutions, but it is essential to allow enough cable to ensure that the light can be moved to the best position, which can change from season to season.

Small gardens offer the perfect opportunity to incorporate some fixed lighting—for example, a built-in banquette or a floating stone shelf over a planter box could have lighting concealed underneath to create a floating effect. Recessed uplights could be buried to uplight the texture of a wall, or lighting could be built into the side of planters to throw light across the path.

RIGHT This relaxed seating area feels warm and welcoming, thanks to the collection of candles on the stone bench, which almost do the job of a fireplace in providing focus. What also helps is the wonderful glow from under the stone bench, created with an external clickstrip or a warm white LED strip that reflects softly off the timber decking.

As with a room indoors, the lighting outside should be controlled by different switches, so that not all the effects have to be revealed at once. Sometimes just the focus of a lit feature at the end of a small garden is enough to lead the eye out.

A purely decorative idea that will add to the ambiance of the outdoor room is to hang party lights in a tree. Anything from three to seven small perforated lanterns, for example, may be necessary, depending on the size of the tree. During they day they look decorative, but at night they provide soft dots of light and can be used in combination with uplights for a magical effect. (See page 157.)

What should not be forgotten is the romance of kinetic light from candles, both on the table and around the edges of a terrace. Torches can also be used in flower beds for added drama. If used beside water, the flames will reflect a wonderful warm light effect.

Top tips for outdoor entertaining

The garden is an outdoor room, and the same rules apply as in a dining room indoors. Begin with the infill light and lighting the perimeters of the garden. Light the beds with a combination of spiked 50W 12V reflectors for a soft wash of light and spotlights for a more concentrated uplight effect under a tree.

Use night-lights in small glass holders as a pretty way of emphasizing a staircase or a low wall and the table.

Focus on the table itself. This can be done using candlelight or, if there is a high tree nearby, locate a narrow-beam spot up to 20 ft. (6m) away to focus a 4-deg. beam on the center of the table.

Other effective features are to stake garden torches into flower beds or pots, especially lining a path, to add an extra dynamic element to the lighting, while an outside fireplace can work well in many garden settings.

OPPOSITE Creating a room outside for entertaining plays on several ideas. Here, one wall of the outdoor dining room is made from tall pots planted with box topiary balls. The LED uplights between the pots work well, as they highlight the sides of each one perfectly, catching on the overhanging sculptural box foliage. The fronts of the pots are left in darkness, so creating a play of light and shadow. The dining table, the central focus of the space, appears to be on a carpet of light. In fact, this is the frosted-glass skylight of the room below. On the table is an arrangement of four night-lights, which provide the central focus.

BELOW This urban garden plays on a screen of colored walls to shelter and protect the dining area. They are staggered to reveal different elements of the garden at different points. The strong shafts of warm uplight at their base are created using low-glare low-voltage recessed uplights. The infill light is created both by the glow from the house (out of view) and by the reflected light from the walls. Again, the central focus on the long table is created by a line of small colored night-lights.

Gardens, decks, and landscaping

The key point to remember is that a little light can go a long way in a garden. Don't over light the outside space, but install sufficient electrical receptacles so that more can be added if required. Control is crucial, especially in large gardens, where not everything should be lit up all the time.

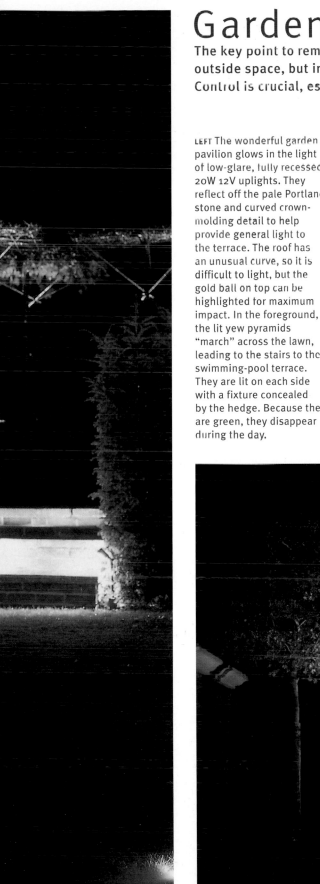

LEFT The wonderful garden pavilion glows in the light of low-glare, fully recessed 20W 12V uplights. They reflect off the pale Portland stone and curved crown-molding detail to help provide general light to the terrace. The roof has an unusual curve, so it is difficult to light, but the gold ball on top can be highlighted for maximum impact. In the foreground, the lit yew pyramids "march" across the lawn, leading to the stairs to the swimming-pool terrace. They are lit on each side with a fixture concealed by the hedge. Because they are green, they disappear during the day.

BELOW Espaliered beech trees form a great visual wall at a high level. Uplight from below emphasizes the wonderful rich russet hues of the changing fall leaves. The area below the trees is lawn, so recessed 35W 12V uplights have been used. If there had been planting around the base, these fully recessed fixtures would be concealed below the planting, so a better choice would be spiked uplights, which can be moved as necessary with each changing season.

Break down the landscape into a series of events and decide how to light each one, starting with the arrival. Brick or stone gateposts will respond well to light and define the entry point. The next stage is to mark the arrival, by uplighting one or several prominent trees at intervals along a long driveway. I think of the trees' shape and size and test various positions before burying a light. A metal-halide source, which comes in two tones of white—cool and warm—is a good choice. A cool color will work best for a pine or cedar tree, as it will bring out the silvery blue of the leaves and needles, while warmer tones will complement an oak or beech tree.

The majority of lighting in gardens should be contained near the house, where it acts as an outside room, just leaving the odd point of focus in the distance, whether a "folly" or a large tree. As indoors, lighting control should relate to each individual area.

When lighting the landscape, it is best to concentrate on structure, as this is easily maintained. Uplighting an avenue of obelisks or topiary, guiding you to an end focus such as a lit sculpture, can be much more effective than random spiked lights in shrubbery. Spiked lights should be kept for areas that are well maintained, usually close to the house. Otherwise, they will be lost in undergrowth. Buried lights are useful in hard surfaces or lawn, but not in flower beds where they will be grown over and lose their effect.

Fountains and other water features respond wonderfully to light. (See page 46.) A brook with bubble jets can appear to have a line of night-lights flickering above the water. In a waterfall, the light needs to be located just below the actual "fall" of water, then it will literally shine through it. Fiber optics are a useful tool to use with water features. The light source is remote, and light travels down a glass fiber and is emitted at the end. If it is used in the spout of a fountain, the water appears to be the light source. (See page 50.)

ABOVE RIGHT The key focus in this seating area is the glow of reflected light off the wood decking, which is created by a warm white LED strip concealed under the stone bench. This is accentuated by the three flickering candles above, which add a dynamic quality.

RIGHT Lighting is all about creating drama and focus, and this avenue certainly does. The eye is drawn along the path by the illuminated stone pillars on either side, reflected on the wet path. At the end, the wonderful jaguar on a plinth is the focus. This is lit by two recessed spiked spots mounted on either side by the last stone pillar and focused on the sculpture. In the background, 70W metal-halide floodlights, with their slightly cool silvery light, catch the trees in the woods beyond. The play of light is the same technique often used in an interior hallway, with the focus on the sculpture at the end, and stepping stones of light leading to it.

Top tips for gardens

ABOVE Lighting trees with uplights creates a wonderful effect, as the light catches the underside of the leaves. Here, a further decorative light effect has been created with starlighters, which are small perforated metal lanterns. The light source within distributes spots of light through the holes. The effect can be magical, even more so when the foliage is blowing in the breeze. Used on their own, starlighters can be a glare source, but when the tree is also uplit, the contrast is less and it almost appears as if the lanterns are doing all the work.

RIGHT These two urns, uplit from the planting below with 12W 20V medium-beam spiked uplights, form the focus. A range of starlighters hangs in a random fashion on the pergola behind them. In the distance, a moonlighter at a high level in a tree creates a cool pool of light on the center of the lawn as it filters through the branches.

Poolscapes

Whether indoors or outdoors, a pool can be lit to create a magical effect. As in bathrooms, lights are rated for use in wet areas. The choice of fixtures also depends on the type of cleaning agent used in the pool.

The tile in a pool can have a big impact on the effect of the light. Subtle dark colors, such as dark blue, green, or slate, create a reflecting pool that blends more naturally with the landscape during the day. If a pale tile is used, the water will be a pale aqua. For a dramatic effect in dark pools, fiber-optic ends can be sealed at random into the bottom of the pool as point sources. These are invisible in the day, but at night the effect is as if a handful of stars has been thrown into the pool. For general light, several smaller light sources are preferable to the traditional large "car headlight" fixtures.

An indoor pool is sometimes an extension of a family room or relaxation area, so its visual impact can still be important when not in use. Make sure that there will be no glare from the pool lights, and consider lighting a focus at one end. If the pool is viewed from the long side with the opposite wall going into the water, light on one side only toward the wall. If the pool is viewed from one end, then lighting from either side is effective. Don't install lighting in the ceiling directly over the pool—this can be impossible to maintain without draining the pool, unless it is done with a fiber-optics starlight ceiling. Instead, consider using wall-mounted lights on each side, which will reflect in the pool when dimmed. (See page 26.)

BELOW This wonderful pool house is reflected in the water. The pool's infinity edge is uplit with fiber optics along the front edge. Rising majestically from either side are two stone urns, lit with fiber optics with narrow-beam lenses set in the bottom of the pool. Their effect is almost ghostlike. Fiber optics were chosen in order to achieve a small source with a remote light box for maintenance. The pool house itself is uplit with 20W 12V low-glare halogen fixtures that reflect off of the curved crown molding, giving light to the terrace. The roof is lit from two shuttered spotlights. In the distance, in the woods behind, a couple of metal-halide sources catch the sculptural branches of the trees in a cool silvery light.

OPPOSITE This double-height indoor pool is lit in a very understated, but dramatic, way. There are no overhead lights, as maintenance would be difficult. Instead, the lighting is reflected off the architecture itself. The pool is lit using small low-voltage LED lights set into the side walls at 5 ft. (1.5m) intervals, producing a more dramatic effect than old-fashioned larger fixtures. Low-level floor washers were recessed into the walls to provide pools of light on the walkway. The smaller windows in the side wall are uplit from lights recessed into the sills using a 20W 12V light source. The large arched windows are lit with 50W 12V sources to create the balance. These architectural recesses allow natural light to flood in by day and become dramatic features, layering light effects and reflecting in the pool at night. Small fiber-optic uplights wash the end wall with soft aqua.

HARDWARE

With increasing concerns about the rising cost and environmental impact of energy production, it is important to understand the effects of the available light sources. Fortunately, lighting technology is developing at a fast rate. Experiment with these new technologies to obtain the best result. There are various tools that are indispensable for achieving versatile and creative lighting schemes, while the fixtures themselves are a personal choice. Here are the most essential tools and some of my favorite light fixtures.

Lighting tool box

Low-voltage recessed directional downlight

This is a useful tool to provide accent and infill general light. With a wide-beam lamp, it can also be used for a wall-wash effect. The key details to check are that the lamp is set well down into the fixture and the baffle is black to reduce glare (some manufacturers use a polished metallic dark light reflector). Ideally, the fixture should also be able to accept different lamps (10–60 degrees) and lenses (softening, frosted, or elongating) to achieve different effects.

Wall-recessed floor washers

Available as round, rectangular, or linear plaster fixtures, they are usually recessed in the wall at a low level (½–1 inch [100–250mm] above the floor), because they have an asymmetric distribution directed toward the floor. They are useful for stairs, corridors, and bathrooms as indicator lights, either using a low-voltage or LED light source. They can also be recessed at a high level (6½ feet [2m] above the floor) for an uplight effect. Make sure the lamp is concealed from direct view, and avoid examples with frosted face plates, because they are not as discreet.

Continuous flexible rope light

Rope light can be a white LED frosted tube that can be curved in various directions. It is ideal for delineation at a low level under a cupboard or for creating a soft effect as a shelf light. There are IP-rated versions for use in wet areas. Others are incandescent and have a clear tube that shows the lamp, so beware of reflections on shiny surfaces. For a higher output, consider using a low-voltage fluorescent source that can be manufactured to almost any shape.

Recessed uplights

One of the most important architectural lighting tools, they are used to uplight columns, archways, window trim, or even plain walls. The light source is either LED, sometimes with a filter to warm up the light and usually with a lens to create a narrow-beam 10–15-degree effect, or narrow-beam low voltage. Be careful with low-voltage fixtures, although their effect is wonderful they are extremely hot to touch; a low-heat version should be selected. (These are usually deep and so are not suitable for all locations.) The key with recessed uplights is to ensure that the light source is narrow and that it is well recessed within the fixture to reduce glare—a lamp near the surface will attract attention and be a source of glare. Avoid frosted glass for the same reason, unless the light source is to be used purely as an indicator light and is of only low output.

Surface-mounted spotlight

These can be used for accent lighting when installing a recessed downlight is impossible. The same rules apply: the lamp should be well recessed within the fixture, and the dark glare should ideally be matte black—if it is white or metallic, it will catch the light and draw attention to itself. Surface-mounted spotlights are often used in converted barns and old houses, where they can be discreetly mounted on the sides of exposed beams to focus on key objects or features. Like recessed downlights, these are most flexible if they can take a variety of lenses and a honeycomb louver to reduce glare.

LED strip

Currently in development, the LED strip improves almost monthly. It uses LEDs at various intervals and can be high- or low-output. The back of the strips get hot, so they need to be mounted on a "heat sink", although they throw little heat forward. The heat buildup needs to be kept to a minimum, as this is one of the key factors in realizing the life and light output of an LED. The key developments have been to achieve a warm white similar to clickstrip, which is a low-voltage

Recessed low-glare low-voltage directional downlight.

Recessed low-voltage or LED floor or ceiling washer.

Wall-recessed low-voltage stair light.

Recessed low-glare low-voltage or LED uplight.

Compact surface-mounted low-glare spotlight.

LED tape light for shelves.

halogen-based mini track that consumes 100W/m rather than the LED's 5–10W/m. The LED strip can sometimes have a diffuser and is used to uplight coves, for both front- and backlighting within shelves, and to underlight furniture. There are versions of RGB (red, green, and blue) LEDs that are able to change color by blending the primary light colors in any combination.

Flush recessed cabinet light

This is ideal for use under kitchen cabinets, for niches, or for lighting objects on shelves. If it is above eye level, always use a small shield to conceal the fixture from view, or select one with a small "eyelid" that will conceal the light source. This can be low-voltage or LED. Always locate the light toward the front edge of the shelf, otherwise it will backlight the object you were intending to frontlight.

Picture light

These useful tools come in many designs. A frame-fixed version is preferable, because then it is located wherever the picture is. When choosing a picture light, avoid contemporary ones that do not project from the wall by at least 4–6 inches (100–150mm), as they will be too close to the picture and light only the top or the frame. Some have a traditional head but a halogen light source, which, with different arm extensions, can light the picture evenly and offer gallery-quality lighting.

Plug-in uplight

Ideal for uplighting a fireplace or corner, a plug-in uplight can be added as an afterthought. Located behind a piece of furniture, it can provide a similar effect to a recessed uplight. The fixture should have a glare baffle, and the lamp should be well recessed, although versions that have the lamp on the surface of the fixture are acceptable if they are concealed behind furniture. Models that use an LED light source are also available.

Plaster wall fixture

This can be painted into the wall and uses a compact fluorescent lamp. Depending on the style of the fixture, the lamp sends light both up and down; slimmer models can only direct the light up. There are versions that have a silk shade in front of the source to create a soft infill light. They are a useful way of introducing a low-energy background light into a room or corridor; they tend to disappear because of their slim profile.

Garden spike

This has a miniflood head, which provides a soft wash to foliage or can be tilted to light a path. Deep olive green is one of the best camouflage colors for use in the garden, making the fixture disappear by day. It is low voltage and requires a remote transformer, which is normally a grouped transformer mounted within 12–16 feet (4–5m) and with a long cable to allow the fixture to be spiked wherever it will create the best effect. This may change from season to season. A spiked fixture offers maximum flexibility, but relies on good garden maintenance to achieve the best results.

Spiked spotlight

This is useful for uplighting trees and garden features, and the copper finish ages well to a brown color. It can be low-voltage or LED, and the remote transformer or driver allows a loose cable for easier final adjustment. Always try to select a fixture with accessories such as a glare cowl. This is often similar to a triangular half-tube that screws onto the front, allowing the source to be concealed from one side and directing light to the foliage on the other. Spiked spotlights are best concealed in low planting, then used to uplight a tree or sculptural feature. If you are using them in a lawn or within pebbles, always select a fully flush recessed fixture.

Eyelid semirecessed low-voltage undercupboard light.

Frame-fixed low-voltage picture light.

Low-voltage adjustable plug-in uplight.

Contemporary plaster up-and-downlight.

Directional spiked garden floodlight.

Adjustable spiked spotlight in a copper finish.

Pendants and chandeliers

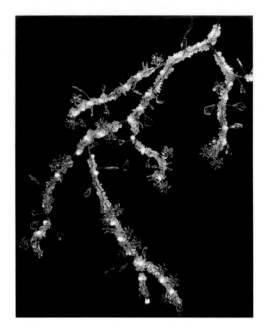

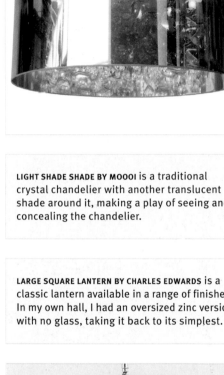

ICE BRANCH BY TORD BOONTJE is part of the Swarovski Crystal Palace collection. It has LEDs interwoven in the crystal branches, which makes it a piece of light sculpture.

LIGHT SHADE SHADE BY MOOOI is a traditional crystal chandelier with another translucent shade around it, making a play of seeing and concealing the chandelier.

BALANCE BY WINDFALL is made up of suspended chandelier elements that can be clustered together or used individually. These are not lit internally, but by a downlight from above.

LIGHT DRIZZLE BY OCHRE is a linear chandelier that is ideal for use over a rectangular table. A separately controlled light source can be used within it to light flowers on the table.

LARGE SQUARE LANTERN BY CHARLES EDWARDS is a classic lantern available in a range of finishes. In my own hall, I had an oversized zinc version with no glass, taking it back to its simplest.

FIL DE FER SOSPENSIONE FROM CATELLANI AND SMITH comes in a variety of sizes. Small capsule lamps are set among the twisted wire, which throw wonderful shadows against a wall.

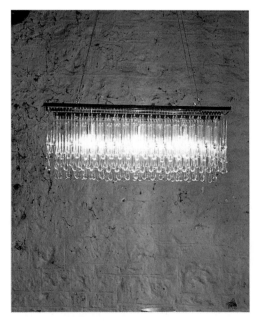

BEAT BY TOM DIXON comes in several shapes, which can look effective hung together over a countertop. The beaten metal has a rustic feel, and the golden interior reflects a warm light.

DECO DISH LIGHT BY CHARLES EDWARDS is stylish in a square room and provides both up and down diffuse light. The pendant comes in different sizes and finishes.

SKYGARDEN BY MARCEL WANDERS FOR FLOS can be suspended over a table. The light within the dome is inset and out of view, illuminating the internal relief decoration of fauna.

CABOCHE BY PATRICIA URQUIOLA FOR FOCSARINI comes in ceiling, floor, and wall-mounted versions. Light is reflected through the glass spheres, with no direct view of the lamp itself.

ARTICHOKE BY LOUIS POULSEN comes in a number of sizes and finishes, including white, bronze, and stainless steel. The light is filtered softly between the flaps, each reflecting it differently.

GLINT LARGE BY CTO LIGHTING has a solid shade that directs light up and down, and a mass of suspended crystals that filter the light. It also works well with a dark shade and gold interior.

Floor lamps

CHANTECAILLE BY CHRISTIAN LIAIGRE is a directional halogen task light that can be adjusted for use as a reading light or to highlight a sculpture or object on a table.

BRONZE STANDARD BY OCHRE This classic in its bronze finish with detail on the stem will look elegant in any room. Bronze can work well in both contemporary and traditional interiors.

LARGE ADJUSTABLE BOOM BY MATTHEW HILTON FOR THE BRADLEY COLLECTION is ideal for use over a sofa. It is cantilevered so its position can easily be altered. A wall-mounted version is available.

GLO-BALL BY JASPER MORRISON is a modular light that looks like a sculpture and glows in all directions, making it ideal for use in awkward corners—for example, in a steeply pitched attic.

CLEAR CRYSTAL LAMP BY SPINA is a sculptural light that would look good used in a pair to frame an entrance. Instead of a shade, strands of crystals hang around the perimeter to diffuse the light.

ARCO BY ACHILLE AND PIER GIACOMO CASTIGLIONI FOR FLOS is a timeless classic. Balanced by the carrara marble base, it can be swung around to change position and its head also rotates.

Table lamps

CHERUB TABLE LAMP BY OCHRE is a lamp at its simplest that will fit into any style of interior. The base is handblown clear glass, and the shade can be any color to suit the decor.

SPUN LIGHT BY SEBASTIAN WRONG FOR FLOS is a classic lamp with a spun-aluminum frame, also available as a floor lamp. It is not ideal beside seating, as it does not produce side light.

MANHATTAN CONSOLE LAMP BY PORTA ROMANA comes in a variety of finishes to suit any interior style. It is large and elegant, and well suited for making a statement in a high-ceiling room.

DITAL BY KEVIN REILLY makes a simple play of parchment and bronze. Its square shape makes it contemporary, yet its finish means that it can work well in some traditional settings.

ANEMONE BY EMILY TODHUNTER has two light sources, one in the shade and the other within the glass base to make each sphere glow. It is part of a collection. (See page 76.)

ANGLE TABLE LAMP BY TOM DIXON Almost more of a task light, this lamp takes minimalism to extremes. The light source is concealed along the length and gives a soft glow.

Wall lights

RUM SCONCE BY KEVIN REILLY is a realistic candle sconce—the "candle" feels like wax, and the bulb is set low in the fixture, making the top glow. There are other designs in the range.

SHADE SCONCE BY KEVIN REILLY is less rustic than the candle sconce. It has a simple metal back plate and a parchment shade that gives a soft light. The range includes pendant fixtures.

UNDULATION NICKEL WALL LIGHT BY WILLIAM YEOWARD is a skinny light ideal for framing an entrance where the space is narrow, and also works between windows or when used in multiples.

FOGLIO BY TOBIA SCARPA FOR FLOS is another classic that produces an attractive up-and-down pattern on the wall. It works well used either on its own or grouped together.

BESTLITE BY ROBERT DUDLEY BEST FOR BEST AND LLOYD was designed in 1930 and comes in various versions and colors. This example is good as a task light over a kitchen countertop.

FLYNN WALL LIGHT FROM PORTA ROMANA is ideal for narrow spaces. The half-shade lights up and down, throwing light on the metalwork that is available in various finishes.

Task lights

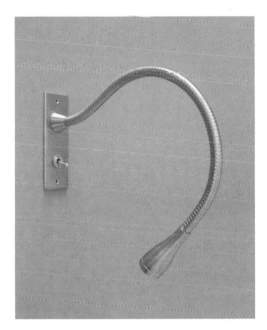

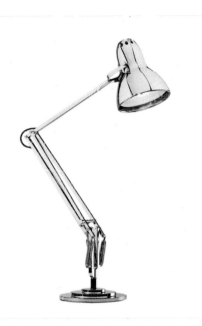

CAMA BEDSIDE READING LIGHT FROM JOHN CULLEN LIGHTING takes a 1.2W LED. I had input into the design, because I wanted a low-heat flexible light so my husband could read while I slept.

ANGLEPOISE® BY GEORGE CARWARDINE was designed in 1934, and it still looks good. The all-time classic is beautifully simple, and new designs take energy-efficient bulbs.

BESTLITE BY ROBERT DUDLEY BEST FOR BEST AND LLOYD is available in various colors. This adjustable version of the classic Bestlight works well as a bedside or kitchen task light.

TIZIO BY ARTEMIDE is one of the first task lights to conceal the electrical power supply to the lamp through the frame itself. The counterbalance action is so graceful.

ARCHIMOON SOFT BY PHILIPPE STARCK FOR FLOS is a wonderful play on a task light. It has a fabric shade rather than a metal one for a softer effect. Also available in a giant version.

KELVIN ADJUSTABLE DESK LAMP BY ANTONIO CITTERIO WITH TOAN NGUYEN FOR FLOS is a clean-lined contemporary Anglepoise® that works well in an office. A low-energy version is available.

Light sources, fixtures, and controls

Incandescent

The traditional general service lamp, which is being phased out in some countries, is the bulb typically used in table lamps. An electric current heats up the filament and produces light. It is hard to beat as a light source, but the quest is on to improve its energy-efficiency and to find an alternative light source.

Halogen

The development of low-voltage halogen light sources in the 1980s changed the face of domestic lighting. The modern solution for every house, it seemed, was to install grids of downlights using these lamps. My view is that the low-voltage lamp has its place, but should be used with discretion and for a particular effect. It still provides the best accent light and is controllable with different beam widths. It has a filament light source, which gives it an element of sparkle that is missing in fluorescent, compact fluorescent, cold-cathode, and LED light sources. It also has the advantage that when it is dimmed its color temperature, which starts off as a crisp white light (3,000K), reduces to approximately 2,000K and takes on a soft candlelike quality.

Fluorescent and compact fluorescent

Recent developments have seen the compact fluorescent lamp (CFL) used as an energy-efficient substitute for a standard incandescent bulb (with a color temperature of more than 2,400K). Manufacturers aim to use this energy-efficient source to re-create the warm light with which we are familiar. Although improving all the time, the problem with these sources is the flatness of light and the fact that dimming is difficult—instead of becoming warmer when dimmed, the light can appear slightly gray. Because of their energy-efficient credentials, it is worth asking your lighting designer to find ways to incorporate these sources.

Metal halide

Another new technology is the miniaturization of metal-halide lamps, which have a powerful light output and low energy consumption. Metal halide requires the lamp to cool down before it can be switched on again, which takes a few minutes and thus limits its use in domestic interiors, but it can be successfully used for lighting trees in the garden.

LED (light-emitting diode)

Energy-efficient LEDs have a long lamp life, low power consumption, and are cool to touch. However, they generate heat from behind, so a good heat sink is needed in order to cool the fixture to ensure the light output remains constant and lamp life is not reduced. LEDs use RGB (red, green, blue) color chips that can be mixed in different degrees to obtain almost any color. The color does not shift when LEDs are dimmed; the light simply becomes less bright. The main effort of manufacturers is focused on trying to achieve a warm-colored white.

The initial whites were too cool (around 5,000K, the color of cool daylight), but a warmer white has been developed (2,700K and 3,000K) to match that of tungsten halogen. New lenses can be used to control the light, so that beam widths, colors, and even the intensity of the light can be changed. To become a true replacement for incandescent lamps, LEDs need to be controllable, so that when they are dimmed their color temperature will be warmer. Increasingly affordable, new strips of LED in a warm color are ideal for lighting shelves and coves. LEDs can also be used as indicator lights for decking or for color-changing effects.

Fiber optics

Here, the light source is concealed in a remote box that sends its light down a bunch of glass fibers. The fibers come in different sizes and are covered in black so that no light can escape from their length. Fiber optics are ideal for use where a remote light source is preferred, such as in a steam room, for a water feature, in display cases where heat would be a problem, or in areas that are difficult to reach and maintain. Care must be taken to keep fiber length the same for an even output of light, and to minimize the length of runs to ensure maximum light output.

Pendants and chandeliers

A pendant usually takes an incandescent or energy-efficient compact fluorescent light source. For a chandelier to sparkle, however, it is essential to use a filament source, which will be reflected in the facets.

Sconces

These can be architectural, sending a beam of light up and down, or decorative, adding to the general light. The light source may be visible in the form of a bar filament lamp in a candle fixture or shielded by a shade. A silk or parchment shade will soften the light and is especially good for disguising a compact fluorescent light source.

Task lights

The most common desk light is the Anglepoise®, and the most popular light sources are halogen or fluorescent, the latter being less hot. For a bedside reading light, a small flexible LED light source is ideal, as it creates very little heat so it is easy to maneuver. In kitchens, task lights tend to be undercabinet lights, and the light source is often low-voltage halogen, which can make the cabinets hot but gives a soft effect when dimmed. Other possible sources are LEDs and slimline fluorescent. If the countertop is polished, a small point source (low-voltage or LED) is preferable to a linear source, which would produce unsightly reflections.

Uplights

When used for background lighting, a linear halogen or energy-saving compact fluorescent source is often mounted on the wall to direct light at the ceiling, which reflects it back softly. Where uplights are used for accent lighting, the light source needs to be narrow and small, as it is likely to be recessed in the floor to uplight an arch or column. Small plug-in uplights need to be baffled to reduce glare. Ideal sources are either low-voltage halogen or narrow-beam LEDs.

Wall washers

These are either track- or surface-mounted, or recessed in the ceiling. The light is directed toward the wall to produce a soft, indirect reflected light. One of the most usual ways to achieve a wall wash effect is with a linear source, such as fluorescent or cold cathode, concealed in a slot. Another typical solution is to use recessed directional downlights with a wide-beam low-voltage lamp and a frosted lens to distribute a wider, softer beam of light.

Recessed downlights

These are recessed in the ceiling and can be used with wide-beam lamps to give general light or with narrow-beam halogen light sources for a spotlight effect. They are useful accent lights to focus on artwork or the center of a dining table, or to use as a task light over a kitchen island. The key is that the light source should be well recessed within the fixture to reduce glare. Low-voltage halogen is used for the small size and flexibility, but in the future LEDs will become a useful source. In utility settings, a fluorescent source can be used in most instances.

Spotlights

These are used primarily for accent lighting in locations where recessed lights are impossible—for example, a barn conversion where spotlights are mounted on beams to uplight the structure or highlight features. When a flexible arrangement is required, a track or wire system (in which the current is carried down a pair of wires, with a transformer at one end) is used. Controllable light sources give the best effect, and the most common is the low-voltage halogen lamp, although LED spotlights are becoming more popular—in particular, for use in display cabinets because of their low heat and compact size.

Strip lights and cold cathode

For a continuous effect, fluorescent is probably the most favored light source, but it must be overlapped to ensure that there will be no breaks. Another option is cold cathode, which is a form of fluorescent that can be custom-made to specific lengths and curves. White and color-change LED strips are increasingly available. Sometimes mini tracks of small low-voltage lamps can be used to create a linear effect. These provide soft warm light, but are very energy-inefficient.

Lighting controls

This is fundamental for achieving mood lighting and ensuring that lighting is used in an energy-efficient way, so that it is on only when

required. The background lighting in each room should be run on a separate circuit to the accent lighting, so it can be used on its own for functional purposes, leaving accent lighting for special effects.

The most basic means of control is, of course, a switch, which can have a dimmer in the back box for more flexibility (new energy-efficient light sources have special dimmer requirements that must be checked with the manufacturer, retailer, or electrician before installation). Local dimmers such as these can be prone to buzzing. Using the standard rotary dimmers means it is only possible to dim at one point and switch off at another, the lights coming on at whatever level they were last set.

Slightly more complicated is a remote dimmer, where the button acts as a signal to bring the light levels up or down. This means that lights can be dimmed at any location, not just one, and the buzzing associated with a dimmer is usually remote, at the dimmer pack. This method of dimming can be frustrating, because if you go past the desired level you will need to work through the whole dimming cycle again.

The next stage is preset or programmed lighting, which enables you to change the lighting scene with each push of the button. The switches or control plates send a signal to the remote dimmers, and the level set on each will be memorized. For example, if there are four remote dimmers, one would operate the decorative lighting, another the uplighting, the third a focused spotlight, and the last the accent lighting for pictures and shelves. Instead of adjusting each dimmer individually, they are all preset at the desired levels.

SCENE I Daytime setting, with decorative lights and uplights, perhaps, but no accent lighting. Lights would not be on where natural light is good.
SCENE II Early evening setting, with the general lighting dimmed and the accent lighting bright, perhaps with a focus in the center of a table.
SCENE III A more dramatic evening setting. In a dining room, this could be the dining setting; in the living room, it may be the party setting.
SCENE IV This is usually the lowest setting, which could be a night-light setting or for watching television in the living room.

Preset lighting with a centralized control system can switch the entire house's lighting on or off automatically, or be set on vacation modes, where different lights go on and off. Such systems can be linked in with the audiovisual and security systems, but need to be installed at the outset. New radio frequency options now exist for retro fit, which can be particularly effective when decoration means that new switch lines cannot be introduced, as the control plate is wireless and battery-operated (the battery works for 3–5 years).

Another control to consider is motion-sensor technology. This can be linked to daylight, so it operates only when it is dark and its level can be preset. Ideal for dressing rooms, some bathrooms, and utility areas, motion sensors solve the problem of lights accidentally being left on. Only use them in the main areas of a home if there is a sophisticated control system that will deactivate the sensor when a mood is selected and will not allow it to work again until the lights are switched off.

A note on energy efficiency

With environmental concerns and the increasing cost of energy, creative lighting must be achieved in an energy-efficient way. Inefficient incandescent lighting used to be favored for its characteristic warm light that becomes even softer and almost candlelike when dimmed. The problem with many energy-efficient sources, such as fluorescent and LEDs, is that while they can be dimmed by special controls, they merely become less bright and do not change to a warmer color, so the light looks almost gray. The challenge is to consider how to use light. Sometimes the answer may be to double up on energy-efficient light sources—for example, to use a cooler fluorescent uplight during the day, and a second slightly filtered source in the evening when a warm light is required. White LEDs can be effective as accent lighting because it is not essential for the focused light to become warm and yellow, as long as the general light does.

How lighting is controlled can also play a part in energy efficiency. Although achieving mood lighting in an energy-conscious way may involve using a greater variety of light sources, the way the lights are controlled can counterbalance this, ensuring that all the light sources operate only when their effect is required. For example, a room that is dull during the day requires a cool light to boost daylight levels, but all the feature lighting would not come into its own until night.

Each country is reviewing its response to energy consumption and new regulations, which either dictate the number of energy-efficient lights to be used or the consumption and have to be taken into account when new buildings are designed. It is not easy to be totally "green," but the creative use of lighting control and careful thought about light sources will allow you to achieve inspirational effects and be energy efficient. Light sources are developing at such a pace that at the point of writing, not all new solutions are available and traditional sources are often combined with some of the new energy-efficient sources, but each day new tools become available.

A note on safety and planning

Before embarking on a new electrical installation, have the existing wiring and fuse boxes checked, as these may need to be updated. Modern lighting techniques require more sockets and power points, and a separate switch line may be needed. Fuses that continually blow are a good indication of an overloaded system. Electricity is potentially dangerous, and for this reason installing wiring and light fixtures is subject to strict safety regulations that must be adhered to. These vary from town to town, so always seek the advice and skill of a qualified licensed electrician.

When undertaking a new installation, consider the following:

1 Ensure that there are sufficient sockets. Ideally, use 15amp receptacles for freestanding lamps and allow 20amp sockets for the television, hi-fi, computer, and so on. Trailing cords may cause accidents, so if possible install floor sockets with flaps in the center of the room for greater flexibility.

2 The positioning of all light fixtures is crucial. Scorch marks can result if fixtures, particularly uplights, are located too near the ceiling or flammable materials. The fixture usually has a minimum safe distance written within its installation instructions, but if it doesn't, consult the manufacturer.

3 Recessed uplights installed in floors should be the low-voltage, low-heat variety, but these can be quite deep to ensure that the lamp is well set back from the surface glass. Other fixtures using narrow-beam LEDs can be successful, again with the light source set back to avoid glare, while fiber optics also offer a solution.

4 If you wish to install recessed downlights, check that there is a ceiling void and how deep this is. It is also important to know what the ceiling is made of, whether standard drywall or a mix of lathe and plaster. The fixing clips of any fixture will need to be checked to ensure they are compatible with the ceiling type. Always choose a downlight with the lamp well recessed within the fixture so that it is out of view and does not cause any glare.

5 Check whether the ceiling void is full of insulation. If it is, clean it out around the position of the light to prevent overheating, or use fixtures rated for insulation contact.

6 Check the position of switches for ease of use.

7 Ensure that any transformers for low-voltage lights or drivers for LEDs are located where they can be accessed for maintenance.

8 For exterior installations, ensure that all cables are mounted well away from any areas that may need digging or mowing. If cables are located in the center of a garden, they should be a minimum of 18 inches (450mm) underground. Check that all equipment is weatherproof and suitable for exterior use.

glossary

BAFFLE Device attached to a light fixture that helps to prevent glare. The light source is set back behind the tube so that it is concealed from view.

BALLAST Adapts characteristics of the electrical supply to suit the lamp; usually used with fluorescent tubes or metal-halide light sources.

BEAM WIDTHS The cone of light produced by a reflector can vary. A narrow beam will have a 10-degree angle, a medium beam a 25-degree angle, and a wide beam a 40-degree angle.

BULBS OR LIGHTBULBS Called "lamps" in the trade, these are the means by which light fixtures are lit up. They take on a variety of effects depending on whether they are clear, frosted, or have an inbuilt diffuser. Incandescent bulbs have a warm light and are usually associated with table lamps; halogen bulbs have a white light and are more often associated with low-voltage fixtures.

COLD CATHODE Generally known as neon, although it can be filled with other gases, such as argon, depending on the color required. The technology is similar to fluorescent, but is easier to control and starts instantly. Available in a vast range of colors. The glass tubes can be made in almost any shape required. Primarily known for its use in signage, but used architecturally to light coffers and coves, and by certain motorists to light under their cars.

COLOR SATURATION The amount of pure color in relation to its brightness. Intense color is often created by using colored light on a same-colored wall.

COLOR TEMPERATURE A measure of the warmth or coolness of a white light source. Paradoxically, the higher the temperature, the cooler the color of light. Expressed in degrees Kelvin; 2,700K is a warm white, while 4,000K is cool. Noon daylight is about 5,500K.

COLOR WHEEL Wheel with various colors, usually used with fiber optics, which allows for a choice of up to six hues.

CONTROL SYSTEM System linked to all lighting that can be manipulated to create effects, such as scene setting.

COWL ATTACHMENT Attachment to reduce the glare from a fixture.

DIMMER SYSTEM Designed to raise and lower lighting levels, combined with an ability to activate preset scenes.

FIBER OPTICS Created by a single light source located remotely in a light box. A special reflector focuses the light down individual glass fibers, usually enveloped in black sheaths, which emit light at their ends. They emit no ultraviolet rays and no heat. Side emitting fibers are unsheathed and continuous light is emitted along the entire length. Sometimes used at the edge of swimming pools to create a continuous effect.

FILTER Usually made of glass, which can be frosted or colored.

FLICKER, SPARKLE, OR SHIMMER WHEEL A mesh wheel, incorporated into a fiber-optic light source, which, when set to rotate, produces a sparkling, shimmering effect. Particularly effective when used with "star" ceilings.

FLOODLIGHT A fixture that creates a wide spread of light; miniature flood fixtures create a similar effect, but are smaller because they use a low-voltage source with a wide-beam reflector.

FLUORESCENT A cool light source from a slim strip of varying lengths. Can be dimmed if an electronic ballast is used, becoming less bright, but not warmer in color like an incandescent source.

FOOTLIGHT FIXTURE Small low-voltage fixture usually fitted to the front of a shelf.

FRAMING PROJECTOR A projector that is concealed within the ceiling, leaving only a small aperture through which light passes. A technician is required to cut a copper mask so that the beam of light exactly frames painting or object. Access from above is needed for maintenance.

GEL Transparent heat-resistant plastic used to add color to a light source.

GLARE GRILLE Attachment used to reduce glare; see also louvers.

HALOGEN A gas introduced around the filament in an incandescent bulb to create a whiter light. Mains voltage or low voltage.

LAMP See *bulb*.

LEDs Light-emitting diodes provide a very low-heat light source with a very long lamp life—around 50,000 hours; usually red, blue, or cool white. These can now be used as an alternative to low-voltage sources for accent lights.

LENS Used to achieve different effects from the same fixture. A spreader lens creates an elongated beam of light when used with a narrow-beam bulb. A softening lens provides a softer wash of light. A frosted lens achieves an even wash of light. A UV lens removes the ultraviolet from a beam and is often used with artworks to prevent fading and aging.

LIGHT BOX See *fiber optics*.

LOUVER An attachment with horizontal or vertical fins, sometimes adjustable, which is directional and reduces glare.

LOW-VOLTAGE A low-voltage lamp fixture operates at 12 volts rather than the usual mains voltage. The advantage of 12V is that the filament in the bulb can be manufactured to a smaller size, which results in a more discreet light source.

LOW-VOLTAGE STRIP A type of track operating at low voltage into which small bulbs can be slotted along its length, either continuously or at intervals. Known as "clickstrip."

MAINS VOLTAGE Any bulb that operates at 230V (Europe) or 120V (USA).

METAL HALIDE Bulb often used in commercial floodlighting. Uses a ballast and provides a cooler light. It is energy-efficient, but cannot easily be dimmed. Used for uplighting trees.

NEON Similar to a customized fluorescent tube. Often colored, it can be made to any shape and is often used in signage.

OFFSET LIGHTING Term used when lighting a building or wall from a distance.

PIR Passive infrared presence detector, which operates a light automatically.
PRESET SCENES Combined lighting circuits programmed to achieve a certain mood where a control system is used.

RECESSED FIXTURE Discreet fixture that can be positioned within the ceiling, floor, or wall. Always flush with the surface.
REFLECTANCE VALUE The proportion of incident light that is reflected by a surface.
REFLECTED LIGHT Light that is bounced off a wall or object.
REFLECTOR Part of a bulb or fixture, and used to direct light in a specific beam. Can be designed to provide either a wide or narrow distribution of light.
REFRACTED LIGHT Light that changes direction as it passes through glass/water.
ROPE LIGHTS A run of small "pea" bulbs set into a flexible rubber covering. Available as low or mains voltage, with a lamp life of around 10,000 hours.

SPIKED FIXTURES Variety of outdoor fixtures with a spike to be inserted into the ground, making them very flexible.
SPILL LIGHT Light that goes beyond the object being lit.
SWITCH LINES Various fixtures that are connected to one switch or dimmer—all the fixtures on one switch line operate together at the same level. Each circuit has a different switch.
SWITCH PLATE Control for switch lines. This could be a "dimmer" or an on/off control. A number of different circuits can be controlled from one plate.

TRANSFORMER Device that reduces the domestic electricity supply from mains voltage to the required low voltage. It can be within the fixture or remote.
TUNGSTEN Tungsten is the filament usually used inside a lightbulb that heats up to provide light. The resulting light is warm and inviting in the evening but can look insipid during the day.

UP-AND-DOWNLIGHT Usually cylindrical wall light that combines spotlights that shine both upward and downward.

WIRE SYSTEM Track with two tensioned cables, powered at 12v, carrying current to small low-voltage fixtures between the cables. The transformer can be at the end of the wires or located remotely.

XENON An inert gas, but in lighting terms it refers to a continuous, flexible lighting system, using small double-ended lamps. Gives a warm light which gets warmer when dimmed. Ideal for domestic cove lighting, but energy hungry.

suppliers

Atlanta

C LIGHTING
333 Buckhead Avenue
Atlanta, GA 30305
404.760.1119
www.cllighting.com

GEORGIA LIGHTING DESIGN GALLERY
530 14th Street
Atlanta, GA 30318
404.875.4754
www.georgialighting.com

VININGS LIGHTING
2810 Paces Ferry Road
Atlanta, GA 30339
770.801.9600
www.viningslighting.com

Boston

BOSTON DESIGN CENTER
On the Boston Waterfront
Boston, MA 02210
617.338.5062
www.bostondesign.com

BOSTON LIGHT SOURCE
64 Commercial Wharf
Boston, MA 02110
617.788.2400
www.bostonlightsource.com

CITY LIGHTS
2226 Massachussetts Avenue
Cambridge, MA 02140
617.547.1490
www.citylights.nu

NEENAS LIGHTING
380 Boylston Street
Boston, MA 02116
617.859.1700
www.neenaslighting.com

SAVIO LIGHTING
280 Worcester Road
Framingham, MA 01702
508.875.8818
www.saviolighting.com

WOLFERS LIGHTING
103 North Beacon Street
Allston, MA 02134
617.254.0700
www.wolfers.com

Chicago

AMERICAN LIGHT
905 West Irving Park
Itasca, IL 60143
630.773.8100
www.americanlight.com

LIGHTOLOGY
215 W. Chicago Avenue
Chicago, IL 60610
312.944.1000
info@lightology.com
www.lightology.com

NEW METAL CRAFTS
812 N. Wells Street
Chicago, IL 60610
312.787.6991
www.newmetalcrafts.com

REMAINS LIGHTING
103 Merchandise Mart
Chicago, IL 60654
312.527.1300
chicago@remains.com
www.remains.com

Houston

AMERICAN LIGHT
5091 Steadmont
Houston, TX 77040
713.462.6258
www.americanlight.com

FERGUSON ENTERPRISES
4245 Richmond Avenue
Houston, TX 77027
252.447.6121
www.ferguson.com

LIGHTINGINC.COM
4218 Richmond Avenue
Houston, TX 77027
713.623.6500
www.lightinginc.com

LIGHTING UNLIMITED
4211 Richmond Avenue
Houston, TX 77027
713.626.4025
www.lulighting.com

M AND M LIGHTING, LP
5620 South Rice Avenue
Houston, TX 77081
713.667.5611
www.Mmlighting.com

Los Angeles

CITY OF LIGHTS
1739 S. La Cienega Boulevard
Los Angeles, CA 90035
310.559.8324
www.cityoflights.cc

FABBY LIGHTING
2611 Exposition Boulevard
Los Angeles, CA 90018
323.939.1388
www.fabby.com

LAMPS PLUS
200 So. La Brea Avenue
Los Angeles, CA 90036
323.931.1438
www.lampsplus.com

LIGHTING EXPO
647 So. La Brea Avenue
Los Angeles, CA 90036
323.938.6026
www.lightingexpoonline.com

MIDWEST LIGHTING SHOWROOM
5250 Hollywood Boulevard
Los Angeles, CA 90027
800.469.3441
www.midwestlighting.com

PLUG INC.
8017 Melrose Avenue
Los Angeles, CA 90046
323.653.5635

REMAINS LIGHTING
765 North La Cienega Boulevard
West Hollywood, CA 90069
310.358.9100
losangeles@remains.com
www.remains.com

Miami

BRAND LIGHTING
2930 SW 30th Avenue
Hallandale, FL 33009
954.456.1006
www.brandlighting.com

FARREY'S
1850 NE 146th Street
North Miami, FL 33181
305.947.5451
www.farreys.com

GOLDENAGE LIGHTING
11441 NW 34th Avenue
Miami, FL 33178
305.718.6698
www.goldenageusa.com

REMAINS LIGHTING
3833 NE Second Avenue
Miami, FL 33137
305.571.2012
www.remains.com

New York

GRACIOUS HOMES
1220 3rd Avenue
New York, NY 10021
212.517.6300
info@gracioushome.com
www.gracioushome.com

LEE'S LIGHTING
220 West 57th Street
New York, NY 10019
212.581.4400
sales@leesstudio.com
www.leesstudio.com

LIGHT FORMS
142 West 26th Street
New York, NY 10001
212.255.4664
info@LightFormsInc.com
www.lightformsinc.com

LIGHTING BY GREGORY
158 Bowery
New York, NY 10012
212.226.1276
www.lightingbygregory.com

THE LIGHTING CENTER
240 East 59th Street
New York, NY
800.417.9860
info@lightingcenter-ny.com
www.lightingcenter-ny.com

LITES ON WEST
511 Canal Street
New York, NY 10013
212.534.6363

MILLENNIUM LIGHTING
152 Clifford Street
Newark, NJ 7105
973.465.8898

MOSS GALLERY
152 Greene Street
New York, NY 10012
212.204.7104

REMAINS LIGHTING
130 West 28th Street
New York, NY 10001
212.675.8051
chelsea@remains.com
www.remains.com

URBAN ARCHEOLOGY
143 Franklin Street
New York, NY 10013
212.431.4646
www.urbanarcheology.com

Philadelphia

KAY LIGHTING & DESIGN
317 Ridge Pike
Conshohocken, PA 19428
800.331.5111
www.kaylighting.com

LIGHTING BY DESIGN
8 Dowlin Forge Road
Exton, PA 19341
610.524.0107

WAGE LIGHTING & DESIGN
401 Bustleton Pike
Feasterville, PA 19053
215.355.1090
www.wagelighting.com

San Francisco

BAY LIGHTING & DESIGN
1140 Folsom Street
San Francisco, CA 94103
415.552.4110

CITY LIGHTS LIGHTING SHOWROOM
1585 Folsom Street
San Francisco, CA 94103
415.863.2020

DJ MEHLER COLLECTIONS
165 Rhode Island
San Francisco, CA 94103
415.864.0850
www.djmehler.com

LAMPS PLUS
4700 Geary Boulevard
San Francisco, CA 94118
415.386.0933
www.lampsplus.com

NOWELL'S INC
491 Gate 5 Road
Sausalito, CA 94965
415.332.4933
www.nowellslighting.com

POLICELLI LIGHTING
2 Henry Adams Street, Suite 320
San Francisco, CA 94103
415.621.7745

Washington DC

THE ANNAPOLIS LIGHTING COMPANY
71 Forest Plaza
Annapolis, MD 21401
410.224.2565
www.annapolislighting.com

BURGESS LIGHTING
10362 Fairfax Boulevard
Fairfax, VA 22030
703.385.6660
www.burgesslighting.com

REMAINS LIGHTING
300 D Street SW, Suite 716
Washington DC, 20024
202.554.2910
www.remains.com

Z FURNITURE
2130 P Street NW
Washington DC, 20037
202.833.3717
www.zfurniture.com

ARCHITECTS AND DESIGNERS

I would like to thank the kind generosity of my clients who let me photograph their homes that I had lit. Also, the wonderful architects and interior designers with whom I worked on these projects. I have listed them below, together with page references of the projects with which they were involved:

CARDEN CUNIETTI LTD
1a Adpar Street, London W2 1DE
Tel: +44 (0)20 7724 9679
www.carden-cunietti.com
Pages 20, 28 top, 49, 60, 61, 65, 68 bottom, 69 bottom, 85 top right, 98–9 and 142

DONALD INSALL ASSOCIATES
19 West Eaton Place, London SW1X 8LT
Tel: +44 (0)20 7245 9888
www.donaldinsallassociates.co.uk
Pages 29 top right, 34, 35 right, 83 right and 145 bottom right

ELLEN FOSTER TAYLOR
Pages 35 left, 50 and 66 bottom

FINCHATTON
25 Ives Street, London SW3 2ND
Tel: + 44 (0)20 7591 2700
www.finchatton.com
Pages 4, 5, 19, 23, 27, 37, 44, 45, 47, 51, 63, 68 top, 69 top, 70, 71 right, 80, 81, 82, 88 left, 95, 106, 111, 114, 119, 127 top right, 128–9, 130 and 140 right

GEORGE CARTER GARDEN DESIGN
Silverstone Farm, North Elmham, Norfolk NR20 5EX
Tel: +44 (0)1362 668130
Pages 46, 48, 148 top, 154, 155, 156 bottom and 158

JONATHAN REED
Studio Reed, 151a Sydney Street, London SW3 6NT
Tel: +44 (0)20 7565 0066
Pages 17, 28 bottom, 29 bottom left, 38 right, 55, 57, 72, 83 left, 88 right, 89, 90 bottom, 91 top and bottom right, 107 top, 120, 125 left bottom, 130 right, 140 top and 141

JULIETTE BYRNE LIMITED IN CONJUNCTION WITH KEITH WRIGHTSON
1 Munro Terrace, Cheyne Walk, London SW10 0DL
Tel: +44 (0)20 7352 1553
www.juliettebyrne.com
Pages 96 bottom, 97, 108–9, 113, 125 top, 127 bottom right and 134 right

LUCIANO GIUBBILEI DESIGN
Studio E6, 71 Warriner Gardens, London SW11 4XW
Tel: +44 (0)20 7622 2616
www.lucianogiubbilei.com
Page 152

NH DESIGN
243–7 Pavilion Road, London SW1X 0BP
Tel: + 44 (0)20 7730 0808
www.nh-design.co.uk
Pages 15, 22, 29 top left, 56, 126 top, 130 left, 133, 135, 143 left, 145 top and 158–9

PHILIP HOOPER AT
Sibyl Colefax & John Fowler, 39 Brook Street, London W1K 4JE
Tel: +44 (0)20 7493 2231
www.colefax.com
Pages 16, 18, 21, 64, 75 bottom, 101, 114–15, 134–5 and 143 right

TAYLOR HOWES DESIGNS
29 Fernshaw Road, London SW10 0TG
Tel: +44 (0)20 7349 9017
www.thdesigns.co.uk
Pages 29 top middle, 40, 41, 43, 58, 62, 66 top, 84, 96 top, 118, 123, 126 bottom right, 134 left, 138, 144, 146 and 157 bottom

THOMAS CROFT ARCHITECTS
9 Ivebury Court, 325 Latimer Road, London W10 6RA
Tel: +44 (0)20 8962 0062
www.thomascroft.com
Pages 2, 3, 16, 18, 21, 64, 75 bottom, 102–3, 116–17, 136–7 and 143 right

TIM SIMOND
Artillery House, 1A Sloane Court East, London SW3 4TQ
Pages 36, 61, 65, 149, 151, 156 top and 157 top

TIMOTHY HATTON ARCHITECTS
The Workshop, 139 Freston Road, London W10 6TH
Tel: +44 (0)20 7727 3484
www.thal.co.uk
Pages 6, 7 14, 15, 22, 26, 29 top left and bottom right, 32, 33, 38 left, 42, 56, 59, 67, 71 left, 75 top, 104–5, 126 top, 130 left, 133, 135, 143 left, 145 top and bottom left and 159

TODHUNTER EARLE
Chelsea Reach, 1st Floor 79–89 Lots Road, London SW10 0RN
Tel: +44 (0)20 7349 9999
www.todhunterearle.com
Pages 24, 31 top, 39, 75 middle, 76, 80, 81, 85 bottom right, 91 bottom left, 107 bottom, 115, 121 left, 122, 124, 132 and 147

TOPHER DELANEY
600 Illinois Street, San Francisco, CA 94107, USA
Tel: +1 415 621 9899
www.tdelaney.com
Page 153

WILLIAM RIGBY ESQ.
Icon Productions Ltd, Oakshott Farm, Hawkley, Hampshire GU33 6LR
Tel: +44 (0)7899 950079
email: will.rigby@hishome.eu
Pages 29 top right, 34, 35 right, 83 right and 145 bottom right

index

Figures in italics indicate captions.

accent lighting 9, 52, 58, 60–5, 71, 73, 105, 109, 112, 115, 118, 128, 162, 171, 172
Adnet, Jacques 91
ambient light see background lighting
ammonite, displayed 66
architectural features 25–6, 25, 26, 27, 42, 52, 94, 134, 145, 147–8
architraves 37, 44, 94, 147
argon 172
Artemide: Tizio 169
attic spaces 138, 139

background lighting 9, 16, 25, 50, 52, 54–9, 73, 87, 94, 110, 118, 122, 128, 140, 163, 170, 171
backlighting 9, 15, 28, 29, 30, 32, 34, 35, 42, 70, 97, 105, 113, 118, 126, 128, 132, 135
backsplashes 110, 112, 113
balconies 16
ballast 172
banquettes 150
bar areas 48
basins, hand 50
bathrooms 19, 60, 69, 73, 74, 77, 130–7
    guest bathrooms 35, 46, 134
Baumgartner, K: A Fitting at de Blausse's 97
beam widths 172
beams 114, 115, 121, 122, 124, 139, 162
bedrooms 19, 74, 122–9
bedside lights 74, 77, 80, 122, 122, 125, 128
Bertoia, Harry 16, 28, 29
Best, Robert Dudley: Bestlite 168, 169
Best and Lloyd 168, 169
Bird, Linda: Feathers 97
"black hole" effect 150
blinds 21, 50, 97, 109, 141
bookcases/shelves 42, 58, 105, 124, 138, 141
Boontje, Tord: Ice Branch 164
box topiary balls 150, 153
Bradley Collection 166
Brown, Don: Yoko X (sitting) 42
bubble jets 60, 156, 157
bulbs see halogen bulbs; lamps (electrical components); incandescent bulbs
Bultman, Fritz 28
buried lights 156

cabinets 110, 112, 114, 132, 163
    Chinese 64, 102
cables 172
candles 118, 118, 121, 150, 153
Cartier-Bresson, Henri 91
Carwardine, George: Anglepoise® 169
Castiglioni, Achille 109
Castiglioni, Achille and Pier: Arco 166
Catellani and Smith: Fil de Fer Suspensione 164
ceilings
    high 64, 64, 77, 78, 98, 102, 110, 112, 132, 132, 142
    low 21, 64, 127, 142
    mosaic 35
    sloping 16, 145, 145
    and uplighting 42
chandeliers 15, 16, 22, 44, 50, 56, 77, 77, 78, 78, 79, 83, 102, 106, 107, 121, 121, 125, 132, 132, 140, 145, 164–5, 170
chimneypieces 30
Citterio, Antonio with Toan Nguyen: Kelvin Adjustable Desk Lamp 169
clickstrips 29, 32, 35, 112, 117, 134, 150, 162–3, 172

"Clicktray" 64
clothes rails 127, 127
coffer lighting 117, 132, 142, 143
cold cathode light source 171, 172
color 32, 32
    color-changing 11
    saturation 172
    temperatures 32, 32, 42, 43, 69, 170, 172
    wheel 172
columns
    downlight 109
    fiber optics 25
    uplit 15, 46, 98
compact fluorescent lamp (CFL) 163, 170
concealed light sources 11, 43, 52, 56, 58, 66–71, 109, 113, 115, 117, 124, 127, 128, 130, 130, 139, 148, 150, 155, 156
conservatories 48, 150
contrast 36, 36
control system 171, 172
Corian surface 110
corridors 21, 42, 48, 142–3
courtyards 60, 147
cowl attachments 172
cross-lighting 37
CTO Lighting: Glint Large 165
cupboards 42, 59, 73, 112, 127, 127
curtains
    continuous light above 4
    highlighting 16
    uplighting 10

decking 11, 150, 156
decorative lighting 52, 76–93
desk lights 73, 74, 74, 138, 141, 169, 170
diffusers 29, 92, 163, 172
dimmers, dimming 10–11, 26, 32, 42, 42, 43, 44, 45, 45, 48, 50, 56, 73, 77, 83, 98, 115, 117, 118, 121, 121, 132, 134, 134, 140, 142, 143, 145, 147, 158, 158, 171, 172
dining areas 118–21, 153
dining rooms 16, 50
display lighting 28, 29, 42, 105
Dixon, Tom
    Angle Table Lamp 167
    Beat 165
doors
    cupboard 30
    entrance 144
    Moroccan 66
    textured timber 30
downlights
    directional 10, 21, 25, 28, 29, 42, 54, 64, 98, 118, 121, 127, 127, 162, 162, 171
    infill lighting 128
    low-glare 16, 40, 44–5, 50, 54, 64, 94, 112, 121, 122, 136
    low-voltage 10–11, 15, 16, 19, 20, 27, 48, 54, 62, 64, 68, 77, 94, 98, 110, 110, 118, 118, 121, 124, 142, 162, 162
    mixed with uplights 9
    narrow-beam 9, 16, 19, 27, 94, 118, 121, 136
    recessed 11, 22, 25, 28, 29, 35, 42, 44–5, 64, 70, 74, 75, 109, 117, 122, 130, 130, 132, 136, 144, 145, 162, 162, 171, 172
dramatic lighting 9–10, 22, 36, 46–51, 142, 143, 145, 146, 147, 148, 153, 156, 158
dressing areas/rooms 56, 74, 127, 127

edge-lighting 9, 48
Edwards, Charles
    Deco Dish Light 165
    Large Square Lantern 164
energy efficiency 172
entrances 48, 146–7, 146, 147, 148

fiber optics 25, 27, 28, 35, 50, 60, 98, 112, 122, 124, 125, 126, 156, 157, 158, 170, 172
filters 172
fire surrounds 38
fireplaces 19, 26, 38, 60, 62, 68, 78, 94, 102, 105, 106, 140, 153
flares 153
Flavin, Dan 93
flexilights 75
flicker wheel 172
floating effect 66, 68, 69, 122, 134, 134, 136, 150
floodlight 147–8, 156, 163, 163, 172
floor washers 20, 21, 25, 25, 26, 38, 42, 66, 94, 105, 117, 122, 130, 135, 142, 142, 143, 145, 158, 162, 162
floors: lights recessed into 8, 10
Flos 165, 167, 168, 169
fluorescent light 25, 29, 35, 43, 46, 48, 56, 58, 66, 69, 70, 73, 82, 93, 110, 112, 113, 115, 117, 128, 130, 134, 136, 138, 140, 141, 141, 170, 171, 172
Focsarini 165
focus 15, 16, 19, 19, 20, 20, 21, 22, 22, 25, 38, 40, 43, 44, 45, 50, 52, 56, 62, 62, 64, 73, 94, 97, 102, 107, 115, 118, 118, 121, 125, 142, 144, 145, 146, 148, 148, 150, 153, 153, 155, 156, 157, 158
footlight fixture 172
footlighters 148
footlights 62
fountains 156
framing projectors 28, 29, 64, 172
fretwork 34, 35
frontlighting 9, 28, 29, 38

gardens 10, 50, 148, 150, 153, 154–7, 172
gels 32, 172
general light see background lighting
glare baffles 163, 171, 172
glare cowls 150
glare grilles 172
glare guards 148
glass
    floor-to-ceiling glazing 108
    frosted 16, 28, 32, 37, 86, 88, 105, 113, 130, 132, 136, 138, 145, 153
    Murano 88
    shelves 28, 37, 48, 69
glow lights 16

half-landings 10, 16, 145
halls 16, 21, 38, 50, 64, 77, 94, 97, 142, 143, 144, 145
halogen bulbs 11, 26, 35, 38, 40, 43, 50, 64, 70, 112, 113, 136, 147, 148, 158, 172
Hatton, Daška: The Waves 105
headboards 122, 125, 126, 128
heat sink 162
Hilton, Matthew: Large Adjustable Boom 166
Hocking, Susan Jayne 84, 118
Hockney, David: Interior with a Lamp 29
home office 73, 121
    see also working areas
Huss, Jean-Marc 118

incandescent bulbs 11, 42, 43, 64, 70, 77, 78, 132, 141, 170, 172, 173
insulation 172
IP rating 130, 132, 135, 158

jackson, Kurt 40
James, Kim 38
John Cullen Lighting: Cama Bedside Reading Light 169

kitchens 54, 73–4, 74, 75, 110–17
    central island 54, 74, 75, 110, 112, 115, 117

Lalique 125
lamps
    Anglepoise® 77, 114, 140, 169, 170
    Arco floor 109
    floor 91, 92, 122, 166
    Flos Arco 88
    "Fortuny" studio 92
    freestanding 9, 10, 21, 74, 88–93, 106, 172
    table 10, 11, 19, 42, 43, 64, 74, 92, 97, 98, 99, 102, 106, 107, 109, 117, 122, 126, 140, 167
    tripod 93
lamps (electrical components)
    capsule 29, 44, 94, 110, 164
    clear 34, 35
    frosted 34
    low-voltage 171, 172
    medium-beam 64, 107, 141
    narrow-beam 48, 48, 69, 71, 107, 109, 121
    pearl 34, 35
    wide-beam 30, 48, 68, 171
lanterns 34, 98, 99, 118, 142, 142, 146, 148, 153, 157, 164
layering 9, 11, 20, 41, 50, 85, 94–9, 106, 134, 136, 142, 147
le Boul, Claude: Poème caché 140
LEDs (light emitting diodes) 11, 21, 25, 29, 56, 58, 97, 124, 147, 164, 170, 172
    clothes rail 127, 127
    and color temperature 43
    dimmed 134
    downlights 28
    drivers for 172
    emits little heat 106
    kitchen 73, 110, 115
    linear LED strip 35
    narrow-beam 172
    reading lights 122, 126
    RGB 32, 32, 170
    in side wall 148
    on stairs 8, 42, 144, 145
    swimming pool 158
    uplights 26, 153, 162, 162
    wall light 125
    warm LED strip 128, 150, 156, 162–3, 162
lenses 172
    elongating 121
    frosted 25, 27, 30, 42, 60, 64, 66, 171, 172
    narrow-beam 158
    softening 28, 172
    spreader 172
    UV 172
Liaigre, Christian: Chantecaille 166
libraries 19, 58, 73, 84, 140
light
    low-level 117
    natural 8, 40, 42, 44, 70, 115, 117, 138, 158
    reflected 54, 98, 147, 153, 173
    refracted 28, 173
light box see fiber optics
lighting circuits 11, 106, 112, 117, 122, 128, 171, 173
lighting tests 26
living rooms 16, 40, 44, 102–9
louvers, glare 115, 172
    honeycomb 118, 121, 136
louvers (parallel slats) 27

mains voltage 172
metal halide 35, 148, 155, 156, 158, 170, 172–3
mezzanine level 109
mirrors 35, 69, 74, 82, 84, 97, 127, 132, 132, 134, 136
mood 40–5

moonlighting 148, *157*
Moooi: *Light Shade Shade 164*
Morrison, Jasper: *Glo-Ball 166*
mosaic *35*, 135
mushroom lights 148

neon 172, *173*
Nguyen, Toan *169*
niche lighting 9, 20, 26, 42, 60, 62, 66, *66*, 69, 74, 125, 127, 130, 132, 134, *134*, 163
nightlights, colored 153

Ochre
 Bronze Standard 166
 Cherub Table Lamp 167
 Light Drizzle 164
offset lighting 173
outdoor entertaining 150–3
outside lighting *109*

Pales, Anna: *Grey Forest 106*
panels, Japanese *122*
pathways 148, *148*, 150, *156*
pattern 34, *35*
pavilions 46, *155*
pendants *4*, 20, 43, 44, 54, 74, 80–3, 98, 102, 106, 112, 115, 118, 122, 125, 143, 145, *164–5*, 170
picture lighting 8–11, *16*, 19, 22, 28, 40, 60, 64, *64*, 105, 163, *163*
piers *48*
PIR (passive infrared presence detector) 134, *171*, 173
planning 172
planting 148, *148*, 150, *155*, 157, 163
Porta Romana
 Flynn Wall Light 168
 Manhattan Console Lamp 167
Poulsen, Louis: *Artichoke 165*
preset (programmed) lighting 171
preset scenes 171, 173

radio frequency control products 11
reading lights 73, *73*, 74, *74*, 87, *92*, 105, 122, 124, 125, 126, 128, *169*
recessed fixture 173
reflectance value 175
reflections 15, *26*, 31, 37, 48, 50, *50*, 58, 59, 60, 64, 66, 66, 69, 74, 75, 80, 88, 94, 106, 110, 139, 157
reflectors 20, *92*, 102, 153, 173
refractions 31
Reilly, Kevin
 Dital 167
 Rum Sconce 168
 Shade Sconce 168

rope lights *29*, 69, 70, 110, *117*, 122, 162, *162*, 173

Safety 172
Scarpa, Tobia: *Foglio 168*
screens 19, 28, 32, 34, 35, 38, *124*
sculptural lights 139
sculpture *16*, 19, 20, *28*, 29, 37, 38, 42, 60, 73, 94, 107, 125, 148, *156*, 156, 163
shades 68, 70, 82, 83, 92, *92*, 102, 121, 122, *122*, 125, 126, 143, 163, 164, 170
shadow(s) 28, *29*, 30, 34, 35, 36, *36*, 37, 38, *38*, 46, 48, 50, 54, 58, *58*, 59, 79, 94, 107, 132, 136, 142, 144, 145, 148, *148*, 153
shelf lighting 4, 9, 11, *15*, 19, 20, 21, 28, *29*, 32, 40, 44, 66, 70, 77, *97*, 105, 114, 150
shelves, glass 28, 37, 48, 69
shimmer wheel 172
showers 66, *66*, 130, 135
side lighting 132, 135, 136
silhouette 28, *29*, 35, 37, 38, 56, 64, 70, 94, 105, 106, 146, 150
sinks 46, 75, 114, *115*, 117, 132, 134, 136
skylights 44, 94, *153*
Smallhorn, Sophie: *No.109 38*
Smith, David *121*
sockets 8, 105, 139, 172
space, enhancing 15–23
sparkle wheel 172
spiked light fixtures 156, 157, 163, *163*, 173
spill light 173
Spina: *Clear Crystal Lamp 166*
spotlights *16*, 29, 30, 38, 48, 64, *98*, 150, 171
 directional *77*
 exterior *148*
 low-glare 127, *162*
 low-voltage 114, *122*, 139, 146, 148
 mini *112*
 narrow-beam 127, 153
 reading *125*
 recessed 9, 20, 64, *64*, 114, 135
 shuttered *158*
 spiked *147*, 148, 156, 163, *163*
 surface-mounted 105, *121*, 139, 162, *162*
 tabletop *107*
stairs
 "dead" area under 26
 glass 25–6, *32*, 42, 144, *145*
 glass-and-metal *105*
 lighting objects on/under *16*
 lit with LEDs *8*, 42, 144, *145*
 spiral staircase *25*
 and wall-mounted uplights 87
stairwells *82*, 145
Starck, Philippe: *Archimoon Soft 169*
starlights 94, *97*, 153, 157

steam rooms *35*
"stepping stones" of light 22, *22*, 48, *156*
steps 147, *147*, 148, *148*
strip lights 25, *29*, 54, 56, 127, *130*, 171
sunshine 37
suppliers 173–4
Swarovski Crystal Palace collection *164*
swimming pools 26, *155*, 158, *158*
switch lines 134, 135, 172, 173
switch plate 173

tables, lighting over *4*, 9, 11, *16*, 20, 42, 44–5, 50, 64, 77, 78, 80, *80*, 98, 105, 106, 107, 109, 115, 118, 121, 150, 153, *164*
task lighting 9, 15, *16*, 42, 54, 58, 72–5, 77, 80, 91, 92, *92*, 102, 105, 109, 110, 112, 114, 115, *115*, 116, 117, 122, 125, 126, 128, 132, 135, *136*, 140, *140*, 141, *166*, 168, *169*, 170
terraces *141*, 147
 roof 50
texture 30, 31
tiling 31, *38*, 115, 130, 132, *136*, 158
Todhunter, Emily: *Anemone 167*
toe kick 112, *115*, 117
transformers 29, 38, 64, 139, 150, 163, 172, 173
trees 146, 148, *148*, 150, 153, 155, *155*, 157, 158, 163
trellis 50, *50*, 150
tungsten halogen *29*, 32, 170

Udell, Patricia *38*
undercabinet light 163, *163*
up-and-downlight 85, *86*, 87, 109, *122*, 143, 144, 145, 163, *163*, 173
uplights 170–1
 enhancing space 15–16
 fiber-optic *19*
 floor 59
 freestanding 105, 121
 halogen 50
 low-glare 94, *147*, 153, 155, 162
 low-heat 36, 66, 144, 172
 low-level 10, 20, 102, 139
 low-voltage 15, 30, 38, *147*, 153, 162, *162*, 172
 medium-beam 60, *157*
 mixed with downlights 9
 narrow-beam 15, 16, 60, 94
 over reveals *8*
 plug-in 8, 37, 163, *163*
 recessed *16*, 19, 26, *26*, 30, 37, 46, 48, 94, 105, 106, 118, 122, 142, 143, 144, 145, 147, 150, 153, 155, 162, *162*, 172
 spiked *157*
 wall 15–16, 59, 87

on wall units *117*
 waterproof 135
urns 22, *157*
Urquiola, Patricia: *Caboche 165*
utility rooms 73

Vanity *130*, 132, 134, *134*, 136
Venetian blinds 21

Wall lights 28, 40, 84, 85, 86, 87, 122, 125, 144, *168*, 170
 with adjustable arms *125*
 crafted *143*
 decorative 132
 entrance 146–7, *146*
 meshed *146*
 metal-shaded *38*
 Moroccan-style *35*
 and pendants 80, 83
 recessed 66
 shallow *145*
 torchière *142*
wall sconces 84, *86*, 168
wall washers 15, 20, 25, 30, 48, 50, 54, 58, 62, 64, 66, 92, 102, 106, 122, 132, 140, 171
wallpaper, silk *30*
walls
 colored 32, *153*
 glass 44
 plaster *46*, 60
 textured 25
Wanders, Marcel: *Skygarden 165*
waterfalls 156
water feature *46*, 156
waterproof lights *130*, 132, 135
Windfall: *Balance 164*
window boxes 16
windows
 alcove *84*
 arched *26*, 84
 bay *21*
 slot 68
wire system 173
working areas 138–41
 see also home office
countertop *48*, 54, 73, 74, 75, 87, *97*, 110, *110*, 112, *112*, 113, 115, *115*, 165, *168*, 170
Wrong, Sebastian: *Spun Light 167*
Wylie, Craig *118*
Wynter, Bryan *107*

Xenon light source 19, 25, *29*, 35, 56, 58, 64, 69, 97, *117*, 134, *136*, 173

Yeoward, William: *Undulation Nickel Wall Light 168*

Acknowledgments

My special thanks to my clients and their designers (listed on page 174) for letting me photograph their homes and gardens, without which the book would not have been possible.

A huge thank you goes to Sarah Roberts, for not only arranging the photographic shoots, but also for patiently typing my longhand script. Also to Saskia Tuke-Hastings in the office for helping to coordinate the corrections, to Zia Mattocks for helping to reword my text, to Lawrence Morton for creating a beautiful book, and to Luke White for his patience and fantastic photography. Finally, to Joanna Copestick and Jacqui Small, for asking me to write the book and share my knowledge.

Picture credits